Contents

DOING THE **RIGHT** THING

10 issues on which Christians
have to take a stand

ROB FROST

MONARCH
BOOKS

Oxford, UK, and Grand Rapids, Michigan, USA

First published in the UK in 2008 by Monarch Books
(a publishing imprint of Lion Hudson plc),
Wilkinson House, Jordan Hill Road, Oxford OX2 8DR
Tel: +44 (0) 1865 302750   Fax: +44 (0) 1865 302757
monarch@lionhudson.com
www.lionhudson.com

ISBN: 978-1-85424-838-1 (UK)
ISBN: 978-0-8254-6176-7 (USA)

Distributed by:
UK: Marston Book Services Ltd, PO Box 269, Abingdon, Oxon OX14 4YN;
USA: Kregel Publications, PO Box 2607, Grand Rapids, Michigan 49501.

Unless otherwise stated, Scripture quotations are taken from the Holy
Bible, New International Version, © 1973, 1978, 1984 by the International
Bible Society. Used by permission of Hodder and Stoughton Ltd. All
rights reserved.

The board and text paper used in this book have been made from wood
independently certified as having come from sustainable forests.

British Library Cataloguing Data
A catalogue record for this book is available from the British Library.

Printed and bound in Wales by Creative Print & Design Ltd.

Introduction – The Frost Debate

Life is so busy and stressful today that people seem preoccupied with coping with the pressures of their own lives and families. There's so much stress at work that many Christians feel they've got nothing left to give to the wider community. I know the feeling! I travel so extensively that when I finally reach home I often want to shut the door and crash out.

As you travel with me on the journey of this book you'll see that God has been challenging me about this. Over the last few years I've gradually been switched on to a whole range of important issues which, I believe, require urgent action from the Christian community.

So – this book is not a bland mix of the different views on contemporary issues. It's written with a heart-felt conviction that these issues need Christians to get involved, make a response, and begin to make a difference!

Of course, there are thousands of other issues about which I could have chosen to write, but within these covers are ten crucial matters for which I personally feel passionate concern. So don't expect some kind of well-balanced 'for and against' argument. This stuff should concern us all, and if we sit back and let the world shape the agenda we've only ourselves to blame.

Nothing was ever changed by people who cared merely about themselves! The world was made better only when ordinary people like you and me seriously invested their lives in the service of the wider community and the greater good.

The truth is that each of us should be making a difference to the society of which we're a part. It's much easier to take care of your own loved ones and let the wider community look after itself – but this isn't what God is calling us to do. A 'carpet slippers' lifestyle isn't a true expression of what it means to be salt and light in the world! I hope that this material will get you thinking, talking and, hopefully, becoming part of a new Christian movement for real change.

You can use this book in two ways: as a personal journey to think through some of the bigger issues of our time; or with a group of other Christians (and possibly others from your local community), as a stimulus for discussion and action. It will be helpful if each person in the group reads the book in preparation for participation in the discussion.

Accompanying each of these chapters is a professionally made TV programme involving a panel of national experts on each subject. The panellists aren't all Christians, so that the discussion has vitality and authenticity. Free download of these programmes is available at the website www.god.tv. You may not want to show the whole show, but you'll undoubtedly find that these programmes will help you to get your own discussion going!

I've enjoyed exploring these issues, making these TV programmes and putting this book together. But at times I've also found it deeply disturbing ... and ultimately quite life-changing. I hope the journey is as challenging for you!

Rob Frost 2007

Chapter One

Doing the Right Thing by the Environment

Global cooling

It was a warm Sunday afternoon when I saw the eco-warriors. I was walking by the River Thames near Kingston when I spotted dozens of them hanging onto the branches of a beautiful line of trees near the riverbank.

The local council had sold the neighbouring land to a developer, and the council had agreed that the trees could be felled because they would obstruct the view of the executive flats about to be built there.

I stood and watched these tree-dwellers for some time. They were certainly having fun! They were calling out words of encouragement from tree to tree and passing crates of beer to each other by a simple system of ropes and pulleys. Meanwhile, on the pathway beneath, eager co-campaigners enlisted my signature for their petition.

The next day the TV news showed the violent scenes of conflict as the police moved in to move them on. Even the TV reporter sounded a note of sympathy as the chainsaws roared and the tall trees were felled. A vista that had been enjoyed for generations was gone for ever.

I've never forgotten that scene and, as I walk the same path by the River Thames now, I always feel a sense of sadness deep within me. The great trees have all gone, and the new exclusive apartment block overshadows the river. It's fronted by some scrawny young saplings that the council has recently planted. I hope that the new flat-dwellers enjoy their uninterrupted view of the river. It came at a price.

I've heard some Christians condemn eco-warriors as subversive or even as enemies of the state. They refute their radical protest as emotive or even dangerous. I beg to disagree. These people are the prophets of our time, just like those Old Testament prophets who were also 'voices crying in the wilderness'.

In some Christian circles 'ecology' has been a dirty word. Shame on us! Those who would protect the planet are loving what God has made and caring about its future. They have been doing what we Christians should have been doing. They have been speaking out whilst we have often remained silent. Many of us have been too caught up in internal church politics to care.

This section of the book was written at a time when I was delivering lectures in a major theological college in the United States. I sat writing in a library where scores of tomorrow's American church pastors were constructing their latest essays and dissertations.

When I enquired at the library's 'info-point' where I might find a section on 'Climate Change, the Environment and Global Warming', the young librarian seemed baffled. After scanning quite a number of digital index files, she eventually beamed 'I've got it.'

I was directed to the top floor of the library, to a stack of books in an obscure area. Some thirty books on homosexuality, and some fifty books on Darwinism and evolution, made me wonder if I had arrived at the wrong place.

But on a half-filled shelf I found a handful of books on green issues and the ecological crisis. It was clear that any theological engagement with this issue didn't rate as having the same significance as that of homosexuality or Darwinism.

Christian theology, particularly in the evangelical constituency within the United States, seems to have had a 'blind spot' to one of the most significant issues of our time. Similar conclusions could have been drawn in the British theological scene up to about ten years ago, but mercifully things have grown apace since then.

The failure of the church to engage with ecology has done great damage to our credibility in the world. Our failure to lead society's thinking and action on these issues has been a damning indictment of our attitudes, exposing both our blindness to a true understanding about our Creator God and our lack of concern for one of the greatest crises of our time.

Political dithering

The Bush government, with its close relationship to many of the evangelical churches in the United States, has been tardy in backing action against global warming. I was shocked to discover how manipulative an influence this administration has been exercising over the findings of some of its own scientific advisors.

The 'House Committee on Oversight and Government' recently heard evidence from eminent American scientists who testified that government officials had 'delayed, altered or dumbed down their findings'.

When NASA scientist Drew Schindell reported that Antarctica may be warming more rapidly than anyone anticipated, his conclusions were watered down and his references to rapid warming were 'deleted by the government'.

Almost 60 percent of US government scientists reported that, over the last five years, their conclusions have been changed or their findings have been misrepresented.

I still meet Christians on both sides of the Atlantic who feel that this issue of climate change has been blown out of all proportion. They support the apparent stance of the Bush administration, that the 'warming period' we are seeing is due to factors other than human activity and that current thinking is just another example of doomsday scenarios recurrent throughout history.

Some Christians even see global warming as a sign of the impending return of Christ, and therefore something which we should actually welcome! This kind of talk drives me to despair, because this interpretation implies that 'doing the right thing' amounts to 'doing nothing at all'!

Many Christians would consider such an eschatological view of climate change to be extreme, but are happy to take refuge in reassurances that there have been several ice ages over the last couple of million years. They quote 'experts' who study past climates and who suggest that the earth goes through an inexplicable warming and cooling cycle every 100,000 years.

Such Christians don't see any connection between human activity and global warming and suggest that it's caused by changes to the earth's orbit around the sun, reversals in deep ocean currents, fluctuations in the radiance of the sun or natural changes in carbon dioxide levels.

Thousands of scientists see things very differently! In 1988 James Hansen, a NASA scientist, told Congress that his research, and the work of a handful of other scientists, indicated that human beings were dangerously heating the planet, particularly through the use of fossil fuels.

Hansen's controversial conclusions set off a political storm, with many governments excusing themselves from lowering the use of fossil fuel, saying that they preferred to wait until more detailed research had been completed.

The United Nations set up a high-powered consultation of scientists and governments, known as the Intergovernmental Panel on Climate Change (IPCC), to report on the progress of that research.

From about 1988 to 1995 the evidence for global warming, though it had been mounting for some decades, remained inconclusive in the eyes of many and was politically disregarded as too insubstantial a theory; but during those years scientists were working quickly to reconstruct the history of the earth's climate and to track its current changes. By 1995, the central research project was complete. The report which the IPCC issued that year asserted that 'the balance of evidence suggests' that human activity was increasing the planet's temperature.

By the time the first of four reports in 2007 was published, however, there was a much more urgent tone. Dr Susan Soloman, one of the two principal authors of the report, told delegates in Paris: 'We can be very confident that the net effect of human activity since 1750 has been one of warming.' The agency concluded that it would have to use stronger language to describe humanity's influence on climatic change than it had previously done.

This IPCC report showed that global warming is being caused by human beings. Instead of the assertion that this was merely 'likely' they moved their findings to 'very likely'. They felt that there was a better than 90 percent chance that the theory about global warming was true.

Some scientists have preferred to take an optimistic view of the future and have tried to estimate how improved technology, energy efficiency and the use of less carbon-containing fuels over the next 100 years could alleviate the problem. But even if we take their optimistic assumptions into account it still seems likely that the amount of carbon dioxide (CO_2) in the atmosphere will continue to go up and up. This process will be accelerated as the booming industrial communities of China and India start to burn fossil fuel in vastly increasing quantities.

Personally, I'm convinced that the linkage between human activity and global warming is significant, and that we choose to deny it at our peril.

At last it appears that the governments of the world are being galvanised into action. Following the publication of the first IPCC report of 2007, the then UK Prime Minister Tony Blair said: 'This is the right moment to look at how we protect our environment and grow sustainably, but also to make sure that we have got secure supplies of energy in the years to come.' He concluded that it was vital that any post-2012 Kyoto process was supported by the US, China and India. We can only hope that this kind of international co-operation will become a reality.

Global warming theory

During the last 250 years the emissions from the combustion of fossilized fuel in coal, oil and natural gas, have sent carbon dioxide, methane and CFC's into the atmosphere.

Scientists believe that this pollution has created a 'greenhouse', or exaggerated heating effect, in the earth's climate, preventing the sun's thermal radiation from being transmitted out to space again as it once was. Instead, it is being trapped, accumulating in the earth's atmosphere, just as a greenhouse interior enhances by containment the warmth it receives from the sun. Sunlight passes through the surrounding blanket of greenhouse gases generated by emissions, and is absorbed by the land, water and biosphere of the earth. The presence of the blanket of gases acts in the same way as the glass panes of a greenhouse, which allow in the light, but trap its energy (heat). Just as in a greenhouse, when the earth in its natural cycles returns the energy absorbed from the sun, the blanket of gases does not permit it to dissipate in the way that it needs to do.

Many scientists believe that this process is already having a catastrophic effect on the world's climate. They don't know how much atmospheric carbon dioxide the earth can tolerate before global warming really takes hold and weather systems are drastically changed.

Samples of the earth's atmosphere, trapped in ancient glacial cores over past centuries, show that the pre-industrial level of CO_2 was 280 parts per million, but that it has increased over the last 200 years to around 368 parts per million, and these levels are continuing to rise rapidly.

This rise in carbon dioxide is of deep concern. Scientists believe it is already leading to an acceleration in global temperatures. The computer models for this process put together just ten years ago are already well out of date.

There are many catastrophic developments produced by this gradual warming-up process. One example is that of the serious consequences resulting from the effect of global warming on the glacial areas of the planet. As the white ice of the Arctic Ocean melts, it no longer reflects the sun's rays back into space as it once did. As this ice turns into water it absorbs more of the sun's heat, and the warming effect is accentuated. Besides this, the thawing tundra is releasing huge quantities of methane, another potent global warming gas, into the atmosphere. These changes not only presage the extinction of the species whose habitat is directly affected, but will also disturb the balance in the currents of wind and wave that determine and stabilise weather patterns in every part of the earth.

By 1995 the theory of global warming began to gain a scientific consensus sufficiently convincing for most of the developed world to be a part of the Kyoto negotiations and the treaty it produced. As a result the majority of the participating nations signed up to ambitious plans for reductions in carbon emissions.

But the consensus didn't extend to the White House, with the result that efforts elsewhere were deeply compromised by the unwillingness of the US government to commit to the necessary reduction in use of energy and generation of emissions.

The IPCC report of February 2007 goes even further than any of the previous assessments. This report concludes that: 'Global atmospheric concentrations of carbon dioxide, methane and nitrous oxide have increased markedly as a result of human activities since 1750 and now far exceed pre-industrial values determined from ice cores spanning many thousands of years. The global increases in carbon dioxide concentration are due primarily to fossil fuel use and land-use change, while those of methane and nitrous oxide are primarily due to agriculture. Warming of the climate system is unequivocal, as is now evident from observations of increases in global average air and ocean temperatures, widespread melting of snow and ice, and rising global average sea level.'

This is sufficient evidence for me! I'm convinced that ecology is an issue for immediate Christian concern and action. It calls for a prophetic response on the part of the church, even if this brings us into confrontation with the powers of corporate business or government. I believe that it's a divine call which we simply mustn't neglect.

The effects on the poor

The effects of global warming are very complex, and will generate multiple serious consequences in every part of the world. One of the best known results is the rise in sea level, a situation which will be made worse in some areas by the withdrawal of groundwater.

As the great ice sheets of Greenland and West Antarctica continue to melt at a faster rate than predicted, there is every likelihood that the rise in sea level will have catastrophic results.

Such a rise in sea level could endanger the world's coastal cities (11 of the world's 15 largest cities are built on estuaries or the coast), inundate prime farmland with water, and drive hundreds of millions of people from their homes (over 70 per cent of the human population of the world lives on coastal plains). There is also likely to be a dramatic effect on water supplies. As some countries become warmer and drier there will be more drought, whilst in other areas flooding will become much more common.

We face the reality that, even if the extinction of species

and the destruction of natural environment do not move us, our species belongs to the whole of creation; what we do to the earth, we do to ourselves – and the first affected, the most vulnerable, will be the poor. The earth can no longer support the levels of consumerism that our affluent lifestyle in the North demands. Basically, the rich consume too much, waste too much and pollute too much.

Some sociologists describe our way of life as a 'technology of death' that defends our privileged position, and makes the poor our victims. In order to survive, the poor are forced to live in unhealthy conditions, cut down forests, kill rare animals and contaminate their water.

Those experts who have been studying the close inter relationship between human and environmental systems are concerned at the effect which global warming will have on the poor.

As global warming causes the oceans to rise, millions of people like those living in Bangladesh will be rendered homeless. But they are not the authors of the problem. It's the affluent people of the world, like us, who have created the clouds of carbon dioxide, who are at fault. The earth could cope with many more human beings with the carbon footprint of the poor of Bangladesh; it cannot absorb the impact of any more adopting a lifestyle like ours.

Computer models suggest that climate change will soon create hundreds of thousands of refugees who will flee rising waters or fields turned to desert.

Those who are most badly affected will soon find themselves living in horrific environments without adequate subsistence for life.

Located just south of the scorching sands of the Sahara Desert is an expansive, semi-arid region of Africa called the Sahel. This sparsely vegetated area receives an average of four to eight inches of rainfall per year during its July to September monsoon season. During this warm time of year, summer rains are usually abundant. But the climate is changing and the Sahel has experienced a devastating drought during the 1970s and 1980s. It has resulted in widespread famine and the loss of more than a million human lives.

Warmer temperatures may seem attractive in some very cold regions, but excessive summer temperatures in areas like the Sahel lead to major health problems, such as heat exhaustion, and a growth in the transmission of tropical diseases like malaria.

Some scientists have tried to calculate the economic consequences of global warming. The costs of coping with this growing crisis are estimated at 1:5 percent of gross domestic product for developed nations and at up to 5 percent for developing countries. They believe that climate change will create as many as 150 million new refugees by 2050, and the poorest will be the hardest hit.

Significant research by Christian Aid and other NGOs concludes that climate change is the most significant single threat to the work of economic development in the poorest countries. Continued global warming will undo decades of progress in fighting poverty. This research has established, beyond doubt, that climate change is not only an issue about the well-being of creation, but a human political issue about poverty and injustice.

Christians must tackle this scandal of rising poverty by working, campaigning and personally altering their way of life to facilitate a reduction in the creation of greenhouse gases. We must support the poor of the world as they deal with the ravages of climate change on their doorstep; in so doing we shall also protect ourselves, for our destiny is bound up with that of the poor.

The causes of climate change lie fairly and squarely at the feet of the rich countries of the world. It is our emissions of CO_2 and other noxious greenhouse gases (GhGs) that are polluting the atmosphere and trapping the radiative force of the sun inside our planet's atmosphere.

If we are to do the right thing, both as committed Christians and as residents of the developed world, we cannot escape our moral responsibility towards the poor of the world. And this means we must be committed to a reduction in carbon emissions and a greener lifestyle.

What can we do?

There can be little doubt that one of our most urgent tasks is to adopt systems of renewable energy, of which solar power is one of the most abundant. Scientists have estimated that there is sufficient production capacity in the world to produce photovoltaic systems (PVs) adequate to provide all the power necessary for the requirements of a world of 10 billion people.

Every hour, more solar energy reaches the earth than the entire world's population consumes from all sources of energy in a year! Unfortunately, it's just so widely dispersed that it's difficult to harness.

Other renewable sources of energy include the wind, biomass (from waste, wood-pulp industry, and corn-derived alcohol fuels), tidal power and geothermal energy (the earth's own heat) – all of which are considered carbon neutral. They, in effect, do not release CO_2 into the atmosphere, but they do produce abundant energy.

Scientists have estimated that in most developed countries big industry and private households could make energy savings of 30 percent at little or no cost. According to the Environmental Protection Agency in the United States, for example, if every American household were to replace one light bulb with a fluorescent energy efficient unit, the energy saved would prevent greenhouse gases equivalent to the emissions of around 800,000 cars.

So we can also do a lot of things ourselves, and such lifestyle changes need to become an integral part of our commitment to Christ. In the UK the gas emissions from cars account for 23 percent of our total emissions, and they grew by a staggering 2 percent in the first six months of 2006.

We need to become aware just how much CO_2 our car emits, and we should consider changing our vehicle for something which is more carbon-efficient. If every vehicle owner in the UK drove just one kilometre less a day we would save 1,300 million litres of fuel a year.

And if we became a little more aware of our use of energy, we could make huge savings. It's estimated that 95 percent of the power we use to charge our mobile phones is wasted because we leave the charger plugged in when the phone is already charged!

It would take a forest the size of 500 football pitches to absorb all of the CO_2 produced by those phone chargers. Similar savings could be made by unplugging the TV, the computer or other domestic appliances when we're not using them.

The average family in the UK throws out 521 kg of rubbish a year. If every household recycled half of its rubbish, the UK's annual CO_2 emissions would fall by up to six million tonnes, as we would save both the fuel used to transport the rubbish and the greenhouse gases the rubbish emits.

After central heating, fridges and freezers are the biggest domestic users of energy, because they are on all the time. Domestic fridge and freezer electricity consumption accounts for some 62 million tonnes of CO_2 emissions per year: about 2 percent of the European Union's total greenhouse gas emissions. If every household in the UK replaced their old fridge freezers with more energy-efficient ones, we would save the equivalent of the output of two typical power stations every year.

And if we all signed up for a green power supply – where the electricity company ensures that for every unit of electricity you use, the same amount of green electricity is generated – a vast amount of CO_2 emissions would be saved.

The food we buy often travels many thousands of miles to

get to our tables and this is a huge contributor to global warming. According to the Institute of Science in Society, food transport accounted for an estimated 30 billion vehicle kilometres in 2002.

A kiwi fruit from New Zealand will have created five times its own weight in CO_2 emissions by the time it arrives in the UK. Eating food that is organic (and therefore produced by methods that pollute less and promote the well-being and diversity of creation), grown locally and in season is infinitely more energy-efficient – and is usually tastier and sometimes cheaper.

A Creator God

There are some who connect the present ecological crisis specifically with Christian teaching, and lay the blame for much of it on the biblical assumptions which lay behind the industrial revolution: that because man is considered to be the lord of creation, he could consume and exploit it as he wished. John White, for example, has argued that our current ecological problems stem from 'a realisation of the Christian dogma of man's transcendence of, and rightful mastery over nature'.

I believe that though the evidence for this view is plentiful, it is a simplistic understanding of the situation. Throughout history there have been Christian leaders who have taught about our responsibility to cherish and care for the planet and exhorted Christians to act responsibly, live frugally, and reverence the wonder of God's creation.

As far back as 1554 John Calvin wrote: 'The custody of the garden was given in charge to Adam, to show that we possess the things that God has committed to our hands, on the condition, that being content with a frugal and moderate use of them, we should take care of what shall remain.'

The Bible teaches that the 'earth is the Lord's', that it is full of God's riches, and that it illustrates his mercy and reflects his glory. Psalm 19 reminds us: 'The heavens declare the glory of God; the skies proclaim the work of his hands. Day after day they pour forth speech; night after night they display knowledge.'

I believe that the world is constantly sustained by our transcendent Creator, He is intimately involved with His creation, He and has given us stewardship of the planet. And it's a stewardship of which one day we will have to give account.

God made the creatures of the earth and of the sea. The Holy Spirit moved over the waters of creation and, at the Father's Word, brought order out of chaos and light out of darkness. Today we are engaged in a massive act of de-creation. We're eroding coral reefs, losing huge amounts of DNA, melting Greenland, and permanently degrading and impoverishing the earth for all who will follow us. And we're doing it for no better cause than to sustain our affluent lifestyle!

The Holy Spirit is the one who is life, who gives life and who renews it. The Spirit is the one who brings freedom, imagination and creativity. It is the Spirit who brings in the new and tunes the discordant tones of creation into the original harmony of God's redeeming purposes. As we work with the Spirit we work to repair and renew the broken world.

The incarnation of Jesus was the divine act which touched the entire universe and brought fresh promise to the world. When Christ came as the suffering Servant, he came to share the brokenness of the planet and to suffer the full force of human and cosmic evil.

He came as the sin-bearer and the trash recycler. He came as the one who takes upon himself the refuse of humanity and he came to bring salvation to all who believe. He came to rise from death, to show that destruction does not have the last word! He came to break the limits of time and space so that he may become the cosmic Christ. 'Behold', says Christ in the book of Revelation, 'I make all things new!'

Several years ago I was in Swansea, researching a novel I was writing called *Hopes and Dreams*. I was working in the University Library, where I began to read about Celtic paganism and then about Celtic Christianity.

The more I read about Celtic paganism the more fascinated I became. Celtic pagan thinking has many parallels to contemporary eco-spirituality. The ancient Celts worshipped the gods in the streams, the trees and the storms. They experienced a powerful connection to the elements and to Mother Earth. They placated the forces of nature with ceremonies and rituals. They spoke of a sense of connection to the powers of the earth which many New Agers still talk about today.

When I came to wrestle with the thinking of the Celtic Christians, I found it deeply challenging. Instead of pointing their pagan neighbours to a 'Creator God out there' they taught of a God who infuses the planet with his life and being. Those who brought the gospel to the Celtic world worked with the understanding, already in place, of a natural order alight with holiness; they baptised the reverence that was already there.

One of the greatest contributions of the Celts to the richness of Christian spirituality was their recognition of Christ in the whole of life. They understood that Christ is not only over all, but in all. His presence suffuses the whole of creation and fills every creative aspect of it, from the majestic to the ephemeral and unseen.

The New Testament teaches that Christ is constantly sustaining all things. 'He is before all things, and in him all things hold together' (Colossians 1:16–17).

I believe it is when our Christian spirituality comprehends that Christ is not only 'out there', but present in every tree and flower and every sunset, that our view of the planet begins to change. A poem by Mary Plunkett (1887–1916) has really helped me to grasp this.

I see his blood upon the rose
And in the stars the glory of his eyes.
His body gleams amid eternal snows,
His tears fall from the skies.
All pathways by his feet are worn,
His strong heart stirs the ever beating sea,
His crown of thorns is twined in every thorn,
His cross is every tree.

I believe that Christ infuses the whole of the created order with His presence, and calls us from a worldly indifference about the planet, to love creation as he loved it and to serve it as he served it.

We need to live our lives in anticipation of the fulfilment of God's Kingdom, and that means preparing the way for His return by caring for what He has entrusted to us. Like servants, we must be busy about our work, so that when the Master returns He will find that all is in order. By caring for the planet we are 'preparing the way of the Lord'. We want Him to be proud of the way we have looked after what is not ours, but His.

Jesus lived a life of simplicity, and He demonstrated what it meant to live a life wholly reliant on His heavenly Father. He calls us to live simply in the same way. For it is through a simple lifestyle that we work for the sustainability of the planet and stand firm against the greedy current of consumerism. Like Jesus, we need to learn how to live in keeping with our basic needs.

Paul taught us so much about hope. It's not a vague kind of wishful thinking that everything will turn out OK; that God will somehow work around our greed and keep the temperature down! This hope involves commitment, sacrifice and the very best that we're capable of.

As we care for our beautiful planet we become partners with the Creator, who every moment is sustaining His created order. In living simply, we become part of that great company working towards the 'new creation' that is coming soon.

Becoming green Christians

Those churches which proudly claim to recycle their bottles or abandon their cars on one Sunday each year are to be commended, but this kind of tokenism falls far short of a credible response to the cataclysmic effects of global warming. We need to model a kind of Christian eco-spirituality that has a burning vision to save the creation; that proves itself in radical and authentic change.

The contemporary church needs to refocus its worship and prayer towards a new awareness of the Creator. Genuine ecological action must flow from the core of our believing, not as a kind of add-on activity that we don't take seriously.

The Revd David Bookless, an Anglican vicar in Southall, was concerned that there was so little 'green space' in his parish. He noted that the Southall Regeneration Partnership Report of 1998 concluded that there 'is a lack of greenery, open space, clean air and environmental awareness – all of which contribute to a lack of confidence and pride in the area'.

He was disturbed by the way that a large plot of land known locally as the 'Minet site' had been so neglected and abused. It had become an illegal fly-tipping site, the home of an enormous unregulated car-boot sale which resulted in tons of litter, and a late night track for local motorbike racing: a muddy quagmire of refuse and waste.

David and his team became key players in the formulation of plans to turn most of the Minet site into a country park which would cater for the needs of both local wildlife and people. After much negotiation and many obstacles to overcome, on 30 May 2002 they eventually gained planning permission for the creation of the Minet Country Park. Gradually a huge group of volunteers was gathered, grants were obtained and the project given solid support from the whole community.

June 2002 saw the beginning of the transformation of the Minet site. David Bookless partnered with the Christian ecology movement A Rocha, and together they produced an Ecological Impact Assessment on the proposed works, for which they were able to act as Ecological Advisors throughout. They oversaw habitat creation and excavation of wetland scrapes, the fencing of areas for the protection of ground-nesting birds, and the removal of twenty lorry-loads of illegally dumped rubbish!

They developed a water trail, they ringed 600 birds of 23 species, and cared for the twenty-two species of butterfly, including the rare Small Copper. Strong links were built with four local primary schools. The team developed a curriculum-linked programme for environmental education, starting after-school environment clubs and holiday play-schemes on the site for 60 local children. They organised family picnics, insect safaris and wildlife walks. The team conducted 23 assemblies in 11 local schools and created resources for a purpose-built floating classroom on the Grand Union Canal beside the site.

It was my great privilege to take part in the official opening of the Minet Country Park. I saw there a parable of redemption, a great witness for Christ, and a sign that Christian mission is credible when it takes our theology of a Creator God seriously. As I meandered around the site that hot summer afternoon, I heard the birds singing and saw skylarks, kingfishers and woodpeckers flying free, where once there had been only rubbish and ugliness to see. The butterflies fluttered through the long grass. A conservationist called me over to gaze with him in wonder at a wild orchid growing by a pond. I looked at the distant line of planes queueing to land at nearby Heathrow and marvelled that even here, near the disused gas-works, this urban wasteland had become Eden reborn.

The Living Waterways project is only the beginning of David Bookless' new ministry with A Rocha UK, and he is already acting as consultant to many other pieces of eco-mission throughout the UK. David Bookless is a contemporary evangelist, taking the Good News of Jesus into situations which many vicars would never get near. His Creation Theology leads to a kind of contemporary Christian lifestyle which draws many committed 'greens' to work alongside him. He is doing much to reclaim the credibility which the church had lost in the eyes of those who love and reverence the earth. Many, in their disappointment at the careless and destructive attitudes they saw in Christians, had turned for spiritual sustenance away from the gospel to earth-friendly New-Age paths of faith; but Dave is witness to a strong and credible Christian eco-spirituality.

And he is not alone. There are other groups, such as the John Ray Initiative, led by a group of eminent scientists with a Christian vision who are encouraging projects enabling Christians to engage with the living earth as an integral part of Christian mission.

As I've travelled the country, I've met Christians who have helped lead Birmingham in Bloom, who are developing prayer gardens, cleaning up rubbish-filled rivers and engaging with the community in practical care of the environment: digging gardens, removing graffiti.

Some of these Christian eco-projects have national or regional impact and influence, but others are very local. The Revd Andrew Knight, a vicar in Sketty, near Swansea, encourages his church to care for the local environment – which may include anything from picking up rubbish to protecting wildlife areas within the parish. He preaches a strong commitment to a Christian creation spirituality.

In missions such as Soul in the City and my own organisation's Dawn Patrol we've discovered that when we take care of the planet in practical ways, and demonstrate a practical commitment to the world around us, we unlock channels of communication which were previously firmly closed. These projects needn't be massive to have a profound effect!

Conclusion

Paul said, in Romans 8: 'We know that the whole creation has been groaning as in the pains of childbirth up to the present time.' But this doesn't absolve us from our responsibility towards the planet. Quite the reverse is true! As stewards we are called to be the midwives at the birth of the new order – positively, practically useful, reliable and wise. Our stewardship of the planet is something for which we will be judged. We need to repent of the way in which we've been living (and 'repent' doesn't mean 'beat ourselves up and feel guilty' – it means 'turn round and head in the opposite direction'). We have exploited and spoilt what God has given us and we have not taken responsibility for looking after it. We need to take a new look at how we live, and make a new commitment to working with the Lord in renewing the planet, which is all part of the redemptive work of Christ on the Cross. Christ's cross stands at the heart of creation, for 'God was reconciling the world to Himself in Christ ... and he has committed to us the message of reconciliation' (2 Corinthians 5:19, also see Colossians 1:20). It is not just for a privileged few, nor even for humanity only, but for every brook and wayside herb, every dragonfly and bee: the whole created order.

Our understanding of creation begins with a new sense that it's God's world and not ours. The choice about how you live in this world is yours, but ultimately, the judgment is His.

Questions for discussion

1 When you read in the Bible '... fill the earth and subdue it. Rule over the fish of the sea and the birds of the air and over every living creature that moves on the ground' (Genesis 1:28), what do you think that means in practical terms about our privileges and responsibilities in the created order?

2 The way to get anywhere is one step at a time. What three steps towards an ecologically responsible lifestyle do you think you could take next at home? And in your church?

3 One of the ways we register our vote for the future of the planet is in the purchases we make. As a responsible shopper, in what order do you rate the following priorities:

a) living frugally – just consuming and wasting less of every-thing.

b) recycling – buying from charity shops; choosing second hand cars, furniture etc; using recycled paper products.

c) buying organic – protecting the earth from too much chem-ical pollution and supporting those farmers who maintain hedgerows and soil quality for generations to come.

d) buying local products – keeping food miles to a minimum, and buying goods produced all in one place, rather than shipped to a new destination for each stage of production.

e) shopping from the catalogues of eco-charities – Friends of the Earth, Greenpeace, RSPB, WWF, Woodland Trust, etc.

4 When the problem of climate change seems so big, and our individual efforts so small, what are your thoughts and feelings about commitment to making a difference?

5 To what extent do ecological considerations determine your daily decisions at the present time?

6 An MP once said regarding redevelopment of land in his constituency 'People are more important than trees'. One of the important functions of trees is to slow down, by their root systems and transpiration, the movement of water through

landscape, protecting against the ravages of both drought and flood. In what ways do you think the well being of animals, plants and humans are inter dependent?

7 Think of a beautiful place where you really felt close to God. Describe it ...

Chapter Two

Doing the Right Thing by the Poor

Recently I was eating breakfast on Euston station. I was engrossed in my newspaper.

He was standing at my table for some time before I realised that he was waiting for a response. I put down my paper and looked up into his unshaven, dishevelled face. He was in his twenties, though he looked old and haggard.

'Got some money for food?' he asked.

My response was immediate and pre-programmed: an automatic defence against intruders into my tightly packed schedule.

'No ... Sorry.'

I picked up the paper again, and in my mind I tried to justify what I'd done. 'It could be dangerous to bring out money; begging on London stations is illegal; he was probably a drunk or a drug addict and my money would be used to feed his habit ... of course I was right to refuse him.' But I felt uneasy and embarrassed.

I peeked around the side of my paper. He had disappeared into the throng of early morning commuters. But I felt distinctly uncomfortable. How could I, a follower of Jesus, turn my back on a human being so desperate for help? What was wrong with me? How could I justify this hardness within me that is so out of step with the Jesus I claim to follow?

When you see a homeless man or woman by the side of the street, or someone thrusts a copy of *The Big Issue* towards you (*The Big Issue* is a campaigning weekly magazine sold by many homeless people), what's your initial reaction? Frankly, I have to admit that mine is to accelerate my pace and to put as much distance between me and the one in need as possible. Yet in my heart I know that this is a person, someone loved by God, and that my response has implications not only for them, but for me.

I excuse myself from concern for the poor by saying that my life is complicated enough anyway ... and by shrugging my shoulders and assuming that I can't actually do anything about it. In such an unfair world there's no way that I can ever really do 'the right thing'.

I know in my heart that Jesus calls me to get past this gut reaction – not to a correspondingly unconsidered response, but to a place of real, practical love. Begging does not bless anybody, and I may decide not to encourage people to approach strangers on the street asking them for money – but it won't do to simply turn away and forget them. I can treat them gently and with courtesy, share with them some-times what I obviously have and they obviously have not and choose to tackle the problem realistically by regularly sup-porting the work of Shelter, or St Mungo's, or the National Children's Home, or the Salvation Army. And though I might not choose to encourage people to beg, I could be sure to buy *The Big Issue* regularly, and properly get to know one of the vendors. I could be generous in my giving to buskers, and all those who are doing what they can to take the first steps up from where they have fallen.

Perhaps even more difficult to contemplate than beggars in the place where we live, global poverty feels overwhelming and becomes a turn-off for many people, Christians included. I'm ashamed to admit it, but it's a turn-off for me. We've all heard the story of those who are hungry, thirsty or homeless, and it's been told so often that most of us have learnt how to protect ourselves from the reality of it. We've become expert in shielding our consciences from any sense of responsibility or practical action.

Over the last few months I have been trying to review my own ability to 'do the right thing'. Has my faith become a form of privatised religion that's just about worship and experience? Has my faith lost its cutting edge over critical issues of social responsibility? Has my Christianity become a self-centred activity devoid of any sense of care for others?

My experience on Euston station and my preparation for this book have driven me to re-examine my own attitudes and prejudices, and I can only conclude that, hitherto, I have not been doing the right thing in respect of the poor.

The starting point

In re-examining my own attitudes I recognise that my reaction to the poor has been far too focused on gut reactions, emotional responses and personal pity for the poor.

Looking back over the years of coming at the issue from this angle, I have come to the conclusion that it has been the wrong starting point for my response to the poor. My emotions are too fickle and my gut reactions too subjective. If I am to do the right thing for the poor I must begin from a different starting point. I must become engaged intellectually. If I am to 'do the right thing' I've actually got to give some quality time to thinking about who God is and what God wants of me!

I've built up walls that have shielded me from the reality of the heart-wrenching TV documentaries and clever aid adverts. It's time that I moved beyond gut reactions to a greater sense of who God is and what he expects of me. Doing the right thing starts from a serious intellectual quest. It begins with the question 'what is God like?' and moves on to 'what does God want me to do?'

That's a very different entry point from compassion based on emotions.

For when I start with God I go back to the core of my

believing – to the heart of my discipleship, to the essence of what it means to make Jesus Christ the Lord of my life.

I must recognise again that God is love, and that His love is the purest love of all: for this God of love cares about the hungry, the thirsty and the destitute with a depth of compassion that I can't even begin to imagine.

God is holy, just and fair, and He knows that the poor of the world are the victims of the rich. He knows that the systems which bring us prosperity are often unreasonable, inexcusable, and unfair.

What, then, does God want? He wants this suffering and poverty to be eradicated, and those of us who are committed to Him to put things right. He wants us to eradicate the roots of poverty and to care for the poor.

God hears the cry of the poor and knows their suffering. He calls me to hear it too – and to offer my life as a channel for Him to pour out His love in blessing on the poor of the world.

In Proverbs we read that 'he who is kind to the poor lends to the Lord, and He will reward him for what he has done' (Proverbs 19:17).

Compassion for the poor must flow out of my understanding of who God is and out of my experience of His love for me. It does not stem from my knee-jerk reaction to the latest famine appeal campaign.

Until I have seen the world through His eyes and comprehended His limitless compassion for the world, I'm nowhere near ready to do the right thing.

It's when I stand where God stands and see what God sees that I understand just how much He cares for every aspect of creation and every person on the planet. He silently suffers alongside the oppressed and the hungry.

I can't claim to follow Him if I don't understand how He feels. He judges the unjust and sees injustice as sin. I can't belong to Him unless I take on this mantle of justice for the world.

The prophet Isaiah encouraged us to 'Seek justice, encourage the oppressed. Defend the cause of the fatherless, and plead the case of the widow' (1:17).

Because God cares for the poor of the earth, Christians have an obligation to take the trouble to understand His love for them and His passion for justice. It is our discipleship to watch and learn and love the character of God and take note that He blesses those who remember people who are lost and struggling, and His judgment is terrible upon those who turn away and refuse to care for the poor.

God must be the starting point – anywhere else renders us too vulnerable to the ebb and flow of our feelings and the frailty of our emotions.

Moving past the excuses

My attitude on Euston station was shaped by a variety of understandable excuses – all quite credible, but ultimately not acceptable; not because I am obliged to give to everyone who approaches me for money, but because I am called to treat every individual as a human being, and to take the trouble to work out an honest, thought-through and prayed-through response to meet these situations when they arise.

Christians sometimes quote Jesus, 'the poor you will always have with you' (Mark 14:7), as though this were some kind of mantra for permitting poverty to continue.

Jesus also said, 'Depart from me, you who are cursed, into the eternal fire prepared for the devil and his angels. For I was hungry and you gave me nothing to eat, I was thirsty and you gave me nothing to drink, I was a stranger and you did not invite me in, I needed clothes and you did not clothe me, I was sick and in prison and you did not look after me' (Matthew 25:41–43).

We say that poverty is just a fact of life, too big to tackle, just something we have to learn to live with – as though this somehow makes it acceptable!

We blame global poverty on the sinfulness of others, as if this makes it excusable. We say it's down to the ignorance of the poor, implying that it's their fault in some way.

We reason that poverty is the result of a flawed social system, unfair global economics or biased laws, as if it's all the problem of some anonymous 'them' and nothing at all to do with us.

Even as I write, I can hear myself making these excuses and I know that I've been trying to defend the indefensible and to excuse the inexcusable.

It can't be right that more than ten million children die every year from preventable causes. (That's 30,000 a day – or one every three seconds.)

It's indefensible that one billion people lack safe drinking water, or that 250 million children work to feed their families.

God is a God of love and a God of justice. He calls me to act in His name, and to act now – or face the consequences of His judgment. I cannot love Him yet refuse to do what He wants, and I cannot serve Him if I don't love my neighbour as myself.

Poverty is evil and unacceptable; and God judges me for my untenable excuses. I am just one person. I can't do everything that is needed but I can, and I must, do something.

Open my eyes

Over the years I have been privileged to meet the poorest of the poor. Some of these experiences have been the richest and most formative of my life.

As a student I was the barber at a homeless shelter in Manchester (though my hairdressing skills left much to be desired!). Those rough sleepers gave me a glimpse of the path to poverty which many of them had followed. I saw for myself how addiction, family breakdown and life's cruel twists of fate can destroy confidence, determination and human dignity, and send people falling headlong into destitution.

One night I trudged the flashing neon streets of Manila to

visit a refuge for child prostitutes. When a local pastor pushed open the door to the ramshackle refuge and shone his torch around, there were children asleep in every crevice and corner. It was heartbreaking to hear their stories and to see how many of them were the innocent victims of a tragic cycle of poverty.

Later, I worshipped beside a mountain of rotting refuse. Gathered inside the tarpaulin cathedral were the Christians who spend their days scavenging garbage for anything to help them survive. Yet they sang with irrepressible joy!

I visited a village in Kenya where the people were starving. The stench of death hung thick in the air. Yet they still praised God under the low moon in the star-filled sky.

I stayed in a United Nations refugee camp between Ethiopia and Eritrea and queued at the latrines with those with no hope and no future. I struggled to eat the fine meal they had prepared for me from their scraps of rice dished out in line. I felt wretched when they washed my feet when I knew it should have been the other way round.

I ate a paltry meal of clumped rice with twenty children in an Indian orphanage as the flies gathered on the plate before me. And no one knew if there would be food tomorrow.

I still see their faces in my dreams and hear their weeping in my prayers.

These experiences have helped to shape the person that I am. If you have never shaken the hand of someone who is hungry, been to where the homeless sleep, or smelt the stench of poverty, you have not yet lived.

Saying sorry

It's iniquitous that millions of people eke out a living on around 50 pence a day. No Christian should rest easy in the knowledge that while, in the affluent west, we own 20 percent of the land, we spend 80 percent of the world's wealth and manage to consume 86 percent of the world's produce.

Affluent lifestyle creates related expectations, so when we develop an addiction to consumerism we become the authors of our own local problems too. One of the yardsticks for measuring poverty is determining the point at which people are able to participate in society. It doesn't take much wit to see that the more simply a community lives, the greater the number of its citizens who will be able to attain contentment. In Britain, where the price of basic accommodation is driven up beyond the reach of a large percentage of ordinary people, and where towns and work requirements are planned in the expectation that everyone in the community will own and drive a car, a situation is created that automatically shunts many citizens in the direction of experiencing poverty quite needlessly. There is so much hidden poverty in Britain; a direct by-product of the expectations of an affluent society. This manifests not only in street-dwellers and beggars and squatters, or in people who have given up hope and taken refuge in alcohol and drugs, but in a myriad quiet, respectable, unremarkable lives lived in private desperation – without drama, but haunted by constant anxiety and a pervading sense of shame, with a hold all too precarious on what little they have, and prospects of unremitting self-denial as a constant feature of life. These people, the unremarkable, uncomplaining, invisible poor, are there in every church community, and their struggle is the direct legacy of affluence and consumerism; it is the reign of Mammon that Jesus said is incompatible with the kingdom of God.

There are many reasons for poverty, to do with history, natural resources and the evils of drought, disease or disaster.

But there are other reasons, too: our expectations for our standards of living, financial systems which benefit us, and the greed which drives our lifestyles.

Many Christians have a clear idea about personal sin: what it does to us, to those around us and to our relationship with Christ. Fewer recognise the implications which flow from the sin of the global economy or the sin of the supermarket where we shop or the banking systems in which we invest. Sadly, many of us are just too lazy or too apathetic to discover why.

Yet this discovery lies at the beginning of doing the right thing.

For if we continue to support that which is destroying others, we must shoulder our responsibility and take our share of the blame.

We are part of the problem of poverty because of what we buy, what we invest in, how we vote and how we live. If we are to do the right thing we must question the systems which keep us in the affluence to which we have become accustomed.

We need to say sorry to the poor of the world. And we need to mean it, for true repentance implies that we are ready and willing to change.

Political involvement

Political action is a godly and Spirit-filled activity. Recently I visited the Foreign Office in London to make representation on behalf of people of Eritrea. As I moved from the security zone and into the august hallways of the Foreign Office I was moved that the British 'head of mission' of that country had spared the time to see me.

I was expecting a somewhat robust and short-shrift kind of reception, but I encountered a man who was willing to listen and eager to help. Too often we forget that there are people of conscience in the corridors of power who could do so much more if they had sufficient support from ordinary people like you and me.

You could organise a petition, see your MP, write to a Government minister or demonstrate outside Parliament – but making representations on the part of the poor is an integral part of doing the right thing. You could also get involved at a local level by finding out what your local council is doing. Perhaps you could stand as a councillor?

The great burden of debt we've placed on the poor nations has done irreparable damage to the development process, and countless thousands have died as a result.

In the global economy there is room to write off many of these debts. In some cases three times the original loan has already been paid in interest charges. The prosperous nations could have done so much good by declaring a biblical season of jubilee and writing off these mountains of debts.

Those Christians who have not backed the Make Poverty History campaign have missed a great opportunity to speak out for justice and to speak up for God. It's still not too late to get behind a movement which has been one of the signs of God's kingdom in our age.

HIV/AIDS

When I was speaking at a conference in Kenya recently, all of the speaking team were asked to have an AIDS test in order to create the right environment for all of the attendees to have Aids tests as part of the conference programme.

In parts of Africa the social stigma of having an AIDS test is such that many men carry the disease into their families. As I received the 'pre-test counselling' the nurse insisted that I talk through the implications to my marriage, family and ministry if I should be found 'positive'.

In fact the test was negative, but I understood for the first time what kind of devastating effect this disease could have on my life and on the lives of those closest to me.

HIV/AIDS is the biggest disaster facing the developing world, because of the huge numbers involved. If love and justice are at the heart of our understanding of who God is, then we must reach out to all who are stricken with this disease and fight for their just right to treatment and care, and work for education about the way the disease is spread and how it may be contained.

The thousands of children rendered orphans by this disease need practical care. Many of them have already contracted HIV and we must invest in their long-term support.

We need to speak out to governments who refuse to accept the reality of HIV/AIDS in their own communities. We need to speak out to drug companies who refuse to provide retrovirals at an affordable cost. We need to publicly challenge those Christians who refuse to support AIDS charities because of their moral sensitivities.

Free trade and fair trade

Many Christians support the concept of free trade. 'After all,' they say, 'a free market allows a fair price to be charged and the natural laws of supply and demand to operate.'

This might seem like a good idea, but at the ground-level free trade is often a tool of oppression and a system which drives local farmers into poverty and starvation.

International loans from the International Monetary Fund, for example, were given to the Ghanaian government on condition that it imposed free trade and ceased giving financial subsidies to farmers. This one condition has resulted in the importation of cheap foreign food produce into Ghana and the redundancy of hundreds of Ghanaian farm workers.

The trade justice movement seeks to speak up for local people in such situations, and to highlight exploitative practices which destroy local businesses and eradicate local employment.

The greedy enterprises of the developed world can destroy the very businesses which are fostering most local initiative and the best local development.

Sometimes trade restrictions are themselves the problem: for instance, the extreme poverty in which English fishermen live – and they, ironically, have to leave fish in their own waters to be caught by other nationals because of European

Union regulations. The argument for completely free trade is not without merit – it at least opens opportunity for those with the will and the drive to promote and protect their own interests and those of their communities.

Sometimes though corporations desperate for new markets sweep aside the businesses which are enabling local families to move out of their destructive cycle of starvation and poverty. That's why we need to protect those struggling fruit farmers and small entrepreneurial co-operatives which are so vulnerable to the arrival of subsidised food produce and dirt-cheap mass produced goods. If we buy locally from small family farms it strengthens the whole local economy; if we buy from large corporations we ultimately export wealth from a community.

We need to question that relentless pursuit of the bottom line at the expense of social responsibility and good business ethics. We need to rein in those international corporations who must monopolise every market, no matter what the human cost involved.

The biblical laws about gleaning (see Leviticus 19:9–10) created a system where people were free to get rich but not to take every last thing – initiative and hard work and co-operative effort were rewarded, but with a certain humility that did not forget those who struggle. The Bible recognises the special needs of the widow, the orphan and the alien. It is still a good rule of thumb today.

Trade Justice, unlike free trade, is a movement which aims to create a fair trading system across the world. Shame on us that the talks at the World Trade Organisation have stalled; shame on us that our elected representatives choose to pursue only those trade agreements which benefit us; shame on us that we have stacked the odds in favour of ourselves by giving most votes to the wealthy nations.

This isn't just a matter of concern for politicians and corporate executives. We can use our own purchasing power to make a huge difference in the world. As individuals we should look at what fills our supermarket trolleys and measure our own commitment to the poor by our weekly shopping list. Do we pick up the cheapest product off the shelf or spend those extra few pence to buy things which are fairly traded?

The impact of this kind of 'people power' on the super-markets has been incredible! What started as a small campaign to help tea pickers and coffee growers is now a mass movement which influences supermarket policy.

If we believe in a God of love and justice, we must become committed to a way of shopping which connects us to the needs of those who supply our supermarkets. For example, when you shop, make sure each item you choose has at least one positive attribute – is fair-traded, or is produced in your country (thus benefiting both the environment and those struggling here), or is from a local family business (benefi-cial for keeping wealth in the local community rather than exporting it to a small group of shareholders), or is from a charitable foundation.

We can only hope that this fair trade movement rapidly extends to change the sweatshops of India and Asia, so that those who make our shirts, shoes and suits are paid fair wages.

Many impoverished communities are being transformed by the fair-trade system, and all for a matter of us paying a few pence more. Justice is nothing if it doesn't affect our everyday decisions at the checkout.

Let me end this section with a caveat. This is a more complex issue than it first appears. Supermarkets and mass production *both* create *and* alleviate poverty. The poor in Britain, and elsewhere in the developed world, could not possibly afford to shop from organic farmers or buy jumpers produced by British artisans, because the poor rely on super-markets. All too probably the dairy farmers whose low income is seen as scandalous cannot afford to shop anywhere other than at the supermarkets that squeezed their margins in the first place. All things are relative. The price of accommodation in Britain means that a wage that looks like riches to an African does not go far enough to buy all-ethical shopping. We each have to make realistic choices. That does not mean we should not aspire to buy wisely.

Child sponsorship

Some Christians struggle with the ethics of child sponsorship; saying that it can create tensions between sponsored and un-sponsored kids. Other Christians say that by focusing on individual children some charities are stooping to emotional manipulation and to a form of fundraising which uses children inappropriately.

I beg to differ. Having visited the work of Compassion, one of the primary agencies in this field in Haiti, I can vouch for the integrity of those involved. By linking individual sponsors with real children, the scale of human need is made more approachable and the possibilities of making a difference more understandable.

The charities involved can show that although the individual children benefit from better health provision and education, they also work towards long-term development goals within each community that they work with. Often their investment in one child ripples through to the broader community and benefits many others.

Certainly my wife and I have found that the pictures and letters from our sponsored child have made these massive issues about poverty and development more understandable and real to us.

The photographs and thankyou letters have made us feel that we are actually in touch with someone in the developing world. Over the years we have seen that even our small contribution has made a real difference, and though we can't change the whole world we can at least change one life!

Compassion alone is working with 800,000 sponsored children around the world. This means that a lot of lives are being changed for the better. Compassion sponsors children from 3 to 18 years of age as well as supporting a few exceptional young people through university, where they can gain professional qualifications. Many will go on to become national leaders, and will be instrumental in making the kind of positive changes that their countries need.

Learning from the poor

Jesus launched His ministry with the declaration that 'the spirit of the Lord is upon me ... to preach Good News to the poor.' His gospel was not only about personal salvation, but about setting captives free, about releasing debts, and about bringing economic regeneration to his hearers.

Sometimes our perspective on the poor is blurred by our pride. It's a pride which views ourselves as somehow better, more educated or more cultured. This pride reveals our own paucity of understanding of God's love. It proves that we are still far from His kingdom ourselves.

The truth is that I have much to learn from the poor. Many of the poor people I have met around the world have a much clearer understanding than I do of what is important and what is ultimately of value. They exemplify qualities of courage and faith which I have never had to find.

God forbid that my charitable donations are just salving my conscience; God save me from caring for the poor just to make me feel better

If I really belong to a God of love and justice I need to find a greater humility. My disdain for the poor heaps God's judgment on me, for the haunting truth is that in His kingdom, the first will be last.

Ultimately the poor have much to teach me, and while I may be reluctant to admit it, God hangs out with the poor, God speaks to the poor and God comes to me in the guise of those who are hungry, thirsty, naked and in prison.

Sadly, if I miss them ... I may well miss Him.

Discussion Questions

1 What are your reactions when you see someone begging in the street? And how do you feel about buskers and *Big Issue* sellers?

2 In what ways do you think we can practically help individuals who have been reduced to begging, without at the same time encouraging begging as a way of life?

3 Look up Proverbs 19:17; Proverbs 30:8–9; Isaiah 1:17; Matthew 25:34–40. What do these verses say about the importance of our attitude to the poor?

4 Have you had to live through any times of serious poverty in your own life? Can you think of someone you know at the moment who is struggling with real poverty? How have these experiences changed your view of life?

5 What are your own thoughts about the spread of HIV/AIDS? To what extent is the spread of the disease about morality ... about poverty ... about education ... about the accessibility of medical treatment?

6 Every time we spend money, we are choosing to support one source of supply rather than another. What are the factors that help you to decide where to shop? In what ways might the way we spend money express our allegiance to Jesus?

7 Thinking now of real people you have met in your life ... some rich, some poor ... remembering them ... What did you learn from them? What might they have been able to teach each other?

Chapter Three

Doing the Right Thing in a Multicultural Society

Early in 2007 it was my privilege to take part in a march organised by the black majority churches of Peckham and Brixton. There had been a spate of teenage shootings in the area, and some local church leaders made an emotional appeal challenging Londoners to walk for peace, and to pray publicly for a cessation of the violence.

A few days later well over 2,000 people turned up to take part outside Peckham library. Sadly, there were very few white Christians on the prayer-walk. It's an event that I would have been disappointed to miss. I found myself linking arms with my black brothers and sisters as we walked down Brixton High Street shouting 'Put down your guns, pick up the Bible,' and, as I did so, I wondered where all the white Christians were!

Car horns blasted in support, people streamed out of supermarkets and barber shops, upstairs windows were flung open and the citizens of Brixton clapped and cheered. I felt uplifted and exhilarated, yet disappointed that this was such a monocultural event. I was disappointed that my white Christian friends had failed to support the black churches and hadn't recognised the significance of what they were doing in taking a stand for peace in violent days.

In hindsight, I wondered whether, had the event been organised by the white churches, the situation would have been reversed and the walkers would have been predominantly white with a small group of black supporters. As an event organiser in London for over twenty years I have found an inherent mistrust between those who lead the black majority churches and those who lead the white churches. We simply don't turn out to support each other, a prime example of actions speaking louder than words.

The late Philip Mohabir was one of the few Christian leaders who made it a priority to build links across the ethnic divide. I will never forget my interview with him on Premier Radio, in which he described the treatment which he received when he first arrived in the UK from Sri Lanka many years ago.

He told me how he had visited church after church in the capital looking for a spiritual home, but again and again discovered a form of racism which had shaken his faith to the core. On several occasions he was politely asked not to come back next Sunday simply because of the colour of his skin. Of course, some churches were notable exceptions to this kind of racist behaviour, but unfortunately Philip didn't find one to welcome him when he most needed it.

Philip went on to form the Afro-Caribbean Evangelical Alliance, and was one of the earliest pioneers of the black majority church movement in the UK. He never lost his gracious care for white church leaders, and was always one of the first to offer support and help whenever a multicultural mission or inter-church project was discussed.

Philip's experience of life in Britain was set against the backdrop of the docking of the ship called the *Empire Windrush* in Tilbury in 1948 and the acceleration of immigration in the 1950s and 1960s. There was enormous suspicion of black migrants, and there can be little doubt that many Christians demonstrated racist attitudes. At the end of my radio interview with Philip he said, 'I sometimes wonder how things might have turned out if the white churches in the UK had opened their arms to their black brothers and sisters who migrated here. A great opportunity was missed.'

'Birds of a feather flock together' is, sadly, often a true description of human behaviour. We can feel vulnerable and out of place in situations where we are greatly outnumbered by those who are different from us. Whether we recognise it or not, we can easily put up barriers against those who are different to us, particularly when we feel confident and 'in the majority.'

But God is colour-blind, and Jesus was incarnate in every race and culture. Paul wrote: 'Here there is no Greek or Jew, circumcised or uncircumcised, barbarian, Scythian, slave or free, but Christ is all, and is in all' (Colossians 3:11). Any debate about immigration, multiculturalism or ethnic conflict must be set in the context of God's perfect standard of equality for all peoples everywhere.

There can be no racial superiority in Christian believing or practice, for there is none in the kingdom of God. All racism is sin. Even if we act out of those cultural prejudices in which we were reared, there can be no excuse for racial intolerance. Sadly, many of us, and I include myself in this, are just too blind to see how offensive our behaviour can appear. Our worldview has often been shaped by a kind of arrogance which is deeply displeasing to God.

Welcome the stranger

My great-aunt had laboriously researched our family on my father's side over many generations. At last she had finished it, and there it all was, laid out before me on a crumpled sheet of A4 paper.

I was fascinated to discover that my family were once immigrants to Britain. Before that they lived in France, but came under the influence of John Calvin's protestant movement and discovered personal salvation through Christ alone.

They, like many others who found this kind of Christian experience, were soon accused of heresy against the Catholic government and the established religion of France. A general edict urging the extermination of these Huguenot Christians was issued in 1536.

As the number and the influence of these French Reformers increased, so did the hostility against them from the Catholic Church and the French State. In 1562, some 1,200 of these Huguenot believers were killed at Vassey. After 1685 this persecution grew stronger, and hundreds of thousands of Huguenots fled France for their lives and sought refuge in other countries.

My own family fled to England. Since the Huguenots of France were in large part artisans, craftsmen, and professional people, they were well received here. Historians believe that their character and talents in the arts, sciences, and industry proved a substantial loss to French society and that England gained much from their hard work and enterprise!

If the people of England in the 17th century hadn't been so welcoming to my ancestors, who knows what my family tree might have looked like! They might have been killed in France, and I might well not be alive today. Sadly, however, British society hasn't always been as welcoming to those seeking safety and refuge here.

British history is full of stories of racism. In 1188 the clergyman Gerald of Wales described the Irish as 'barbarians', saying that they 'live like beasts'. In 1218 Stephen Langton, the Archbishop of Canterbury, forced all Jews to wear a badge of white material so that they could easily be identified, and within seventy years Edward I had banished all Jews from the country. This shameful ban would last for 300 years.

In 1562, under the patronage of Elizabeth I, Britain's first slave trader, a man named John Hawkins, sold 300 West African men to planters in Haiti. It was the beginning of a disgraceful practice that continued in the British Empire until 1834. When it ceased, the slave-owners were given £20 million in compensation, a vast sum; but the slaves got nothing.

In 1905 the Aliens Act was passed to keep 'Britain for the British'. It was designed to keep out Russian and Polish Jews who were fleeing persecution. In 1962 the Commonwealth Immigrants Act was introduced following the race riots of 1958. This was an Act which aimed to control the number of new immigrants coming into the UK because they were felt to be responsible for the problems to do with lack of housing, job shortages and rising crime.

Immigration continues to be an intensely political issue, and our ports of entry seem more daunting to immigrants than ever. Even those who come to the UK on legitimate business can be harassed at their point of entry to this country.

I spent over six hours at Gatwick Airport one hot July day trying to get a Mexican student into Britain. She was coming to do voluntary youth work in the Isle of Man as part of a programme of mission and cultural understanding. She had been to the British Consul, had all the paperwork that had been requested of her, and was in possession of several letters of invitation from British church leaders.

Her flight had been delayed by tropical storms, and after being awake for twenty-eight hours she was subjected to a further six hours 'in custody' at Gatwick. The main bone of contention from the airport immigration officials, bizarrely, was that 'we have no previous evidence that the Methodist Church does good work, and it is not registered as one of our charities that performs such a function, and thereby have no evidence that this young person will do good work during her stay here.'

When I heard that the young lady was to be bundled onto the next flight to Mexico in her exhausted state I was speechless with indignation. Fortunately two Members of Parliament and an excellent immigration solicitor went to extraordinary lengths to help me. I spent much of the day on my mobile phone, and it was a very stressful experience.

It was only when the officials at Gatwick heard that they were being summoned to a judicial review on the subject of the 'good works of the Methodist Church' that my Mexican student was suddenly released with many pleasantries and apologies.

How far have we come from the biblical entreaty which urged the people of Israel to look kindly on those who came to settle among them? 'When an alien lives with you in your land, do not ill-treat him. The alien living with you must be treated as one of your native-born. Love him as yourself, for you were aliens in Egypt. I am the Lord your God' (Leviticus 19:33).

Whilst I support an immigration policy which protects national borders and controls migration, I believe the present policies have led to a ridiculous level of bureaucracy and many who should be welcomed, particularly for short term educational opportunities or for conferences or meetings, are being turned away unnecessarily. The concept of 'strong borders' has gone too far. People coming here on legitimate business should be welcomed, and those seeking to come to study or work here should be given every encouragement to do so.

It's even more crucial that those who are fleeing persecution, oppression or violence should be received with warmth and hospitality. After all, these are the characteristics of a civilised society and the marks of a humane culture.

A report by the British Foreign Policy Centre has recently argued that the emphasis on the obligations put onto migrants coming into the UK is 'obscuring the duties of host communities to welcome newcomers', and warns that forcing people through a painful arrival process makes them less willing to integrate.

The report concludes that those 'who are made to wait indefinitely, who are given little information or who are treated disrespectfully will clearly be less willing to adapt and cooperate with the integration process.' I couldn't agree more, and can only hope that these concepts will be translated into normal immigration practice.

It's time we properly welcomed those who fit the agreed criteria, giving them the kind of immediate support which will stimulate integration rather than segregation. There can be no more poignant exhortation about this than the words of Jesus in his judgment of the sheep and goats when he said 'when I was a stranger you welcomed me.'

I have lived in the UK all of my life, and have always been proud to be British. I don't mean a kind of jingoistic pride which is all about nationalism and flag-waving, but a quiet confidence that the way we do things is usually right. We have a high regard for human rights and deep down we are a caring kind of people.

All these former preconceptions, and my unwitting complacency, changed for me at 4am one Thursday morning, when about nine police officers arrived at the home of a neighbour of mine. The children, aged 10, 12, 15 and 17, were herded into the lounge with their parents, who were Kosovan refugees. The police packed one bag for each of them, and they were escorted to Stansted airport.

They were not allowed to make a phone call: not allowed to call their solicitor – not even able to tell their next door neighbour what was happening. They were just whisked off into the night. 'You can make a phone call at the airport', they were told, but on arrival this permission was withdrawn.

'Can we see our solicitor?' they asked. The authorities replied 'No, he's too busy for you'; a comment which outraged their solicitor, for I know full well that he would have made time to respond at whatever hour of the day or night. 'Don't worry', the children were told, 'you'll be given a nice house where you are going.'

On arrival in Kosovo they were told that, unfortunately, there were no houses left. So this vulnerable family, in a state of deep shock, were dumped in a town twenty-five miles from the airport with no place to go. In the end they had to live in the lounge of a relative. Six more people, in a house already full to overflowing.

'Ah, but they were just asylum seekers,' some might respond. 'They were over here as economic migrants.' 'They were spongers, claiming off the welfare state.' 'There are just too many, we can't cope.' 'It's their hard luck, they shouldn't have come here in the first place.'

I live in Wimbledon, a very middle class British suburb of South London. I had imagined that some of my neighbours might subscribe to these kinds of sentiments, but in fact my phone was white-hot with people from all over the area who, hearing of this family's plight, were saying 'I'm ashamed to be British.'

Perhaps our neighbours had learned something of this family's arrival here. They were brought here for safety by the British government after six months hiding in the woods, the children scared and traumatised. They'd seen members of their family assassinated before their eyes. When the time came for their asylum hearing, their state-aided solicitor failed to turn up the first time and went to the wrong court the next. And when, eventually, he did put in an appearance, he knew practically nothing about their case.

I was able to engage a new solicitor for the family, who prepared carefully for their next hearing; but he had not been informed of their impending deportation. As I accompanied this family through the appalling process of seeking asylum, I was shaken by the the institutional racism I discovered in the various authorities, and horrified to witness the unthinkable poverty they endured whilst living in one of the richest nations on earth.

We were able to secure the services of a child psychologist from a major London teaching hospital, who flew out to Kosovo to see them. His report established that the repatriation of those children to the place where they had been so traumatised had done them immeasurable damage.

The Sunday evening after they were deported, three seats remained empty at our church in Raynes Park – the places normally occupied by the three older children who were sent back to Kosovo. In deep silence forty young people gathered for church. None of us felt much like worshipping. It was like coming to a funeral. We mourned the loss of our friends, but it went deeper than that. We felt we had lost something intangible. Our confidence in the nature of the society to which we belong, and in the authorities who are over us, had died.

It cost thousands of pounds in legal fees, a church-led demonstration which was featured on radio and TV news, and a legal team from Cherie Blair's law firm to get this case taken seriously. Finally, with one week to go before the High Court case was to be heard, we got them back.

They were flown back to Stansted, the only occupants on a 150 seat plane (which had been packed with deportees on the way out). And as they re-entered through immigration the officer told them, 'Don't worry, we know where you are. We'll get you back out to Kosovo soon.' To his disappointment, I suspect, their appeal was upheld: they were allowed to stay.

Whether we like it or not, there is institutional racism in many areas of our public life. The population of the United Kingdom now stands at just over 60 million, of whom about 4.6 million (8 per cent) come from an ethnic minority background. That includes 2.3 million people who describe their background as Asian, 1.1 million who are Black Caribbean or Black African, and nearly 700,000 of mixed race.

Despite the fact that this group makes up a sizeable proportion of the UK population, they suffer ongoing physical and verbal abuse. There was a 28 per cent increase in prosecutions for racially aggravated offences in 2006 and further significant increases in 2007.

A review by Sir Derek Wanless, former chief executive of a leading UK bank, has revealed that black children are five times less likely to be registered as 'gifted and talented' than white children, and three times more likely to be excluded from school.

The proportion of non-white people who run into difficulties with the law indicates that there may well be something wrong with the system. Home Office data shows that black people in Britain are six times as likely and Asians twice as likely, to be stopped and searched by the police as white citizens.

Research also indicates that black and Asian people are more likely to be imprisoned than white defendants – and, if found guilty, are likely to receive longer sentences. Twenty per cent of those who are in jail in the UK come from an ethnic minority community – whilst they make up only 8 per cent of the population. And 10 per cent of non-white people have had their details added to the national DNA database, compared to only 5 per cent of white people.

Old prejudices die hard and racist attitudes still lurk deep in the hearts and minds of many of us. Those Kosovans are my friends. I have come to know them and to love them. They will bring much to our country in the years to come, and now that they have their British passports they are immensely proud of the nation which gave them shelter, and of the community which has given them a place they can call home. I felt proud that, despite everything, the British justice system had upheld that which was fair.

Immigration has become a politicised and emotive issue, and Christians need to be counted among those who speak up for the oppressed, who question policies which are driven by prejudice and racism, faithfully upholding and representing the best of British cultural traditions of fairness, justice and respect.

Has multiculturalism failed?

It's little wonder that people arriving in the UK gravitate toward those who speak the same language, eat the same food and live by the same cultural norms. I have to admit that in my extensive travels around the world it's sometimes been comforting to go to a burger bar or to stay at a western-style hotel, because the familiarity of western culture in far-away places can be strangely reassuring.

For generations a pattern of monocultural communities has developed in the UK, allowing incomers the familiarity of living among others of their own kind. Some areas have become outposts of Dublin, others the suburbs of Jerusalem; some are full of shops from Mumbai or lined with restaurants from Islamabad. These ethnic communities have offered friendship, affirmation and healing to new immigrants from their own culture.

The British government over the last thirty years has welcomed this trend, and it has seemed politically correct to recognise such communities as an enrichment to our island nation. The unwritten code has been 'live and let live'. We have been persuaded that we should allow these cultures – be they African, Caribbean or European – to develop and prosper in all their richness.

My work as a minister has taken me to British streets where the smell of curry and the sound of the muezzin fills the air, and to areas of London where the wide brimmed hats and coat tails of traditional Jews fill the street on Sabbath eve. I've eaten in English Chinatowns which made me feel as though I were in the Far East, and been the only white person worshipping in inner city Caribbean churches where rice and peas followed the morning worship.

Recently our multicultural policy has been called into question, however. The rise of militant Islam, the threat of terrorism, and increasing racial tension in schools have required our leading politicians to think again.

Many have begun to question the policies of successive British governments in encouraging monocultural communities to take root. A recent BBC poll revealed the concern in the public mind over these matters, when it demonstrated that 58 percent thought that 'people who come to live in Britain should adopt the values and traditions of British culture'; 32 percent believed that these monocultural communities 'threaten the British way of life' and 54 percent thought that 'parts of the country don't feel like Britain any more because of immigration'.

The BBC newsreader George Alagiah has said that multiculturalism in Britain is creating segregated areas within its cities. He believes that 'a combustible combination' of segregation and deprivation may be fuelling home-grown terrorism. He likened the present situation to 'a garden that has been allowed to run wild'.

Britain's first black Archbishop, the Rt Revd Dr John Sentamu, Archbishop of York, made a powerful attack on multiculturalism, urging English people to reclaim their national identity. He said that too many people were embarrassed about being English: 'Multiculturalism has seemed to imply, wrongly for me, that we should let other cultures express themselves without letting the majority culture tell us about its glories, its struggles, its joys, and its pains.'

He continued: 'I speak as a foreigner really. The English are somehow embarrassed about some of the good things they have done. They have done some terrible things, but not all the Empire was a bad idea. Because the Empire has gone, there is almost the sense in which there is not a big idea that drives this nation.'

The Ugandan-born Archbishop, who fled Idi Amin's regime in 1974, said he would not be where he was today were it not for the British Empire and the English teachers and missionaries who worked in Africa. He said that the failure of England to rediscover its culture afresh can only lead to greater political extremism.

Sentamu believes that multiculturalism as a concept has failed to convey the essence of what it means to be English. 'England is the culture I have lived in, I have loved... My teachers were English. As a boy growing up, that is the culture I knew.'

The Archbishop's concerns are reinforced by a significant

report published by the Institute of Public Policy Research. It reveals that 51 percent of ethnic minority citizens call themselves 'British', compared to 29 percent of whites, who prefer to see themselves as English, Welsh or Scottish.

Those who are from ethnic minorities, however, look on themselves as British Pakistani, British Indian or British Black. Those who are identifying themselves in this way are making a statement that they will identify with the flag and legal systems of their host country, but not its historic culture. They prefer to cling on to their own cultural heritage.

The report concludes that this trend points to 'the growing importance of religion and religious identity to younger British Muslims ... This greater sense of Islamic identity and popularity of related cultural attitudes is likely to be a sign of resistance to the current political climate.'

I find this trend deeply disturbing. It seems to indicate a lack of integration by those who are migrating here. We who represent the host country must take our share of the blame for this, and this growing divide between those who see themselves as British and those who see themselves as English, Welsh, Scottish or from Northern Ireland reveals a cultural disconnection which is growing apace.

The Cantle Report, under the jurisdiction of the Home Office, in the wake of disturbances in Bradford, pointed out that housing and schools policies have favoured segregation in the name of cultural integrity and cohesion. Sadly, however, this has had the unforeseen consequence of alienating the different religious, racial and cultural groups from one another.

This Report, called 'Community Cohesion', observed the kind of problems which the emergence of these monocultural communities can cause 'when geographic, educational, cultural, social and religious divisions reinforce each other to the extent that there is little or no contact with other communities at any level. This appears to allow ignorance about each community to develop into fear, particularly when fostered by extremists attempting to demonise a minority community.'

The Cantle Report concluded that it has not always been the wish or intention of minority cultural groups that they should close themselves off from the mainstream of society and end up in a kind of ghettoised community together: 'Some choices are not, however, always freely made and may simply reflect housing policies or the real constraints imposed by the deprivation of some groups or individuals.'

Bishop Michael Nazir Ali, Bishop of Rochester and from Pakistani Muslim family origins, has said that the cultural heritage of people who come here must be respected. They should be able to take pride in their language, literature, art and spiritual background. At the same time, however, Nazir Ali feels that those who settle here need to learn how to adjust to life in this country, and should be prepared to live in mixed communities, not just among their own ethnic group.

Immigration policy in the UK has been adapted over time to take account of possible tensions inherent in uncompromising cultural divides. Recognising undesirable social outcomes, ranging from simple isolation through mutual suspicion to terrorism and racist violence, there has been an increasing political movement towards encouraging and enhancing sympathy for characteristically British views among those who choose Britain as their home. Many asylum seekers come here enveloped in a personal shell of trauma, fear, and loss. Such people inevitably cling to the familiar, but if kindly and respectfully received may be encouraged to integrate with the society which offers them sanctuary. Learning to speak English, and undergoing a course of cultural education in citizenship, may be a helpful way forward in achieving such integration.

Peter Riddell, of the Department of Islamic Studies at the London School of Theology, wonders if the concept of multiculturalism shows evidence of flawed thinking, based as it is on the assumption that all ethnic communities share a common view of cultural equality and subscribe to an equal recognition of the rights and values of others. This optimistic expectation fails to take into consideration the tensions that must arise when the members of any one particular religious group espouse the belief that their way of life is the only right one, and an assertiveness develops which is likely to alienate adjacent neighbourhood communities.

The social imbalance created by reluctance to integrate can be seen in the instance of Muslim presence in a non-Muslim country. In 1980 the Islamic Council of Europe published a book called *Muslim Communities in Non-Muslim States*. It clearly explains the Islamic agenda for Europe. It describes how, when Muslims live as a minority, they face a major theological problem because traditional Islamic teaching always presupposed a context of Islamic dominance. The book lays out guidance as to how Muslims should live in non-Muslim states when they are a minority of the population.

The book instructs Muslims to assemble and to organise, with the aim of establishing a viable Muslim community based on Islamic principles, making it clear that this is the duty of every individual Muslim living within a non-Muslim political entity. They should set up mosques, community centres and Islamic schools and they must consciously avoid assimilation by the majority. It is inherent to Islamic philosophy and practice, therefore, that strong monocultural Islamic communities should develop, and so the basic expectation of multiculturalism, that minority cultures over time will integrate is, in the case of such monocultural faith communities, fundamentally flawed as a proposition, and overwhelmingly likely to meet a significant measure of disappointment. In Islam, as in every religion, there are moderates and liberals as well as fundamentalists, but in times of tension and unrest of whatever cause, difference and separatist fundamentalism will always be enhanced and underscored.

Jonathan Oloyede, a church leader and former Muslim, is concerned that some Islamic young people have become radicalised, now seeing it as imperative that they impose the values of their own community on the host community of which they are a part.

It is of great concern to many of us that support among the Islamic community for the 9/11 and 7/7 terrorist attacks averages 8 percent of the whole group in most polls. While this means that the vast majority most emphatically do not support these attacks, it still indicates that approximately 160,000 British Muslims do so! It is impossible to remain complacent about the threat to public order and peace that is posed by such attitudes in so significant a minority, especially in view of the extreme measures of disruption they may feel driven to employ.

Simon Hughes MP sums up the concerns of many in his inner city constituency which crosses many cultures. 'For the first time in a generation there is an unease, an anxiety, even at points a resentment that our very openness, our willingness to welcome difference, our pride in being home to many cultures, is being used against us; abused, indeed, in order to harm us.'

The wider population has every right to be concerned about cultural groups who are following an agenda which might ultimately damage the host culture. Such an agenda does not fit easily into a tolerant society. Unless the moderate Islamic voice wins the argument, we may expect a serious breakdown of social cohesion. Some believe that social engineering must be used to provide greater integration and understanding throughout the whole population, whatever our faith or ethnicity.

If any community is following an agenda which aims ultimately to take control of the host nation this is likely to lead to social unrest on an increasing scale, and may inspire growing animosity and hatred, resulting in a breakdown of law and order.

Multiculturalism is not a biblical concept. The kingdom of God is an expression of the reign of Christ, who joins us together in a multi-ethnic, multi-coloured, multi-cultural body of love. Jesus crossed cultures, broke down walls and cut through the barriers that separate people. Nothing which separates, divides or creates hostility between ethnic groups can be pleasing to God. It's the building of relationships across cultural barriers which brings glory to God, and which builds His kingdom on earth.

Some have cited the American model of immigration as superior to that which has developed in the UK, pointing to the integration over the last 200 years of a stream of immigrants from all over the world. Many have been assimilated into American society at their own pace, improving their income and social status on the way. The nature of American national identity, with its emphasis on symbolic patriotism, allegiance, national values and a national ethos, has naturally facilitated this gradual assimilation of immigrants.

Those migrating to the USA did not have to learn a detailed knowledge of American history or acquire a complex cultural heritage. US immigration policy has allowed them to retain an interest in the culture of their country of origin, and to keep their family ties with the people of their home country. Some ethnic groups, such as the Irish and Italians in New York, have responded well to such an approach, assimilating the American way and becoming part of the 'American dream'. In practice, their original culture virtually disappeared within two generations, whilst an americanized version of the original nation's cuisine and holidays has survived.

However, the same approach has not met with equal success for all ethnic groups. The American model of integration has not worked as well for English-speaking, US-born black people, who have significantly failed to thrive economically and in terms of social status and prosperity from the American Civil War onwards.

The massive influx of immigrants from Spanish speaking countries has also proved problematic, with many Hispanic immigrant communities experiencing disproportionate levels of poverty and deprivation. Some areas in Florida and Southern California are now dominated by the language and cultural norms of the Latin peoples. As a result there has been increased racial tension in these areas, with calls for tough new state-enforced immigration policies similar to those that we are now seeing in Europe.

Neither the UK nor the USA style of immigration is perfect. It is the challenging task of government to maintain a balance of co-existence that respects and celebrates difference in immigrant groups, while simultaneously requiring thse groups to extend the same courtesy to their neighbours of different ethnic origin. There can be no better alternative than the mixing of the races, religions and cultures in schools and communities; any future vision which accepts division and suspicion as a *de facto* characteristic of society is an admission of political failure.

While faith schools have been welcomed enthusiastically in the UK, with an accolade from the previous minister for education, who said, in 2001, that he wished he could 'bottle their ethos', they also pose certain grounds for concern, be they Christian or Islamic, Jewish, Seventh Day Adventist or Sikh. When we look at the history of Northern Ireland within living experience, we understand how a ghettoised educational system can exacerbate segregation, leading to deepening suspicion between people groups and a breakdown of community life. Faith schools enhance and enrich our society by encouraging a holistic philosophy of education: we welcome their contribution to national life, but must always guard against the possibility of a sectarian approach.

As committed Christians we must learn how to follow Jesus faithfully, retaining a distinctive Christian commitment while working in harmony and partnership with neighbours of many different cultural backgrounds. Jesus speaks to us with the universal language of love and we must learn to speak it too. Multiculturalism has failed us, and segregation must become a thing of the past: integration that incorporates a respect for distinctiveness can be the only way towards a more safe and harmonious future.

The Archbishop of York dislikes the word 'tolerance' when used in reference to people of different cultures. 'It seems that the word "tolerance" is bad because it just means "putting up with it",' he said. 'I was raised in the spirit of magnanimity. That is a better word than tolerance. If you are magnanimous in your judgments on other people, there is a chance that I will recognise that you will help me in my struggle.'

While government money has been spent on promoting cultural identity, and the experiences of my friends from Kosovo make all too clear how vital such promotion has been, in a culture where institutional racism is still apparent when the surface is scratched, there is now a corresponding need to find government funding for the building of real relationships between people of different cultural groups. We must stand up for the equality of all citizens, no matter which ethnic group they represent, for any inequality of treatment can only breed resentment and a breakdown of unity.

We must promote allegiance to the rule of law, and that means that we must resist the emergence of alternative systems of religious law being proposed as a prior allegiance and threatening to drive a huge wedge between different ethnic and faith communities. If one group is living by one set of laws while a neighbouring community is living by another, our sense of corporate unity and nationhood is doomed.

We must educate for responsible citizenship, ensuring that in all our schools understanding and respect for the people of every religion are expected in daily life and taught as a core part of the syllabus.

Finally, we need to agree a common language: an ability to speak the language of the host nation is a vital prerequisite for becoming fully participating citizens in a host community. If we can't talk to one another, how can we possibly integrate?

We must move to a richer relationship with one another than one which is just based on 'tolerance', and it's impossible to do that if we are segregated from one another in ghetto communities without ever taking the opportunity to get to know each other!

Peace and love

Though religious attire holds no personal significance for me, I was deeply concerned to read of the French Government's decision to forbid Islamic girl pupils to wear the hijab in the school classroom. Aimed principally at pupils in state schools, the law extends to a ban on religious symbols, including large crucifixes, turbans and the yarmulkes of Jewish boys.

The intention of the French government was to uphold their national tradition of the separation of the church from the secular state, but President Jacques Chirac and the centre-right government hoped that it would also halt an upsurge of Islamic fundamentalism held responsible for a growing number of attacks on Jewish targets in France.

Opponents argue that the law encourages religious intolerance and forms part of a politically driven strategy to counter Jean-Marie Le Pen's extreme-right National Front party. Le Pen warned France's secularity commission that banning the hijab would be interpreted by many Muslims as a gross insult, fanning the flames of extremism and doing nothing to address the sense of alienation and discrimination experienced in the Muslim population.

There has been corresponding advocacy of similar legislation within the British context. This option for secularisation as a solution to inter-cultural tension seems to be getting stronger and more poignant. Those in the Protestant tradition for whom ritual garments or symbols are not mandatory should not imagine that these matters don't concern us. Any limitation of religious freedom may ultimately be the thin end of a very large wedge.

The European Convention on Human Rights states, in Article 9: 'Everyone has the right to freedom of thought, conscience and religion; this right includes freedom to change his religion or belief and freedom, either alone or in community with others and in public or in private, to manifest his religion or belief, in worship, teaching, practice or observance.'

The wearing of religious symbols is an essential part of our freedom to 'manifest religion in public', in religions such as Sikhism, Judaism and Islam where religious attire is an integral and mandated expression of faith. Though we might not share the religious perspectives or belief-systems of the groups affected by this French legislation, we should still stand with them in the protection of their basic religious rights.

Martyn Eden, formerly political observer for the Evangelical Alliance, has noted that 'in the developed nations, traditional worldviews and the Judaeo-Christian moral consensus have given way to the influence of modern relativism, pluralism, materialism and what is called postmodernity. These cultural changes have given a new slant to the human rights movement and made it threatening to the orthodox Christian faith community in ways not anticipated 50 years ago.'

In the creation passages of Genesis 1 and 2 we see that human dignity stems from the concept that we are created in the image of God. Because of this, all human beings are worthy of respect regardless of their abilities, status, race or gender. In our faith context we believe that all are equally worthy and equally sinful, and we believe that it is God's will that all should be saved. We understand that God created human beings with an innate freedom to choose how they should live, and that, ultimately, we respect the God-given freedom of choice which is an integral part of what it means to be human.

This implies that I must respect the right of others to wear the hijab or the burka, to wear a turban or a crucifix as a witness of their spiritual allegiance, just as I expect to exercise my right to wear an ICTHUS ('fish') badge, or still carry my Bible with me when I am in public. This is what 'a free society' means.

It was my great privilege to meet Miss Eweida, the British Airways check-in clerk who refused to take off her crucifix when she was told that it contravened British Airways uniform policy. I fully supported her campaign, and felt her success to be a victory for common sense.

Christians can't, on the one hand, support Miss Eweida's right to wear her crucifix, but not support the rights of other religious groups to wear symbols which are important to them. If we are to live harmoniously and to see integration of all the different ethnic groups into our society we must stand up for each other's rights, defend each other's religious practices, and ensure an equality of treatment by those to whom authority is entrusted.

Grace and peace

The redemptive power of Jesus goes beyond the politics of human self-interest. I will never forget the gracious words of Gordon Wilson of Enniskillen, praying forgiveness for the IRA, with the dust and blood still on his face from the bombing which took the life of his daughter, and very nearly his own life too.

I spent a morning with him several years later, and heard how much that bold moment of grace and forgiveness had cost him. He was shunned by many of his friends, criticised by some in the churches, and condemned by those who thought he'd forsaken 'the Protestant cause'. It cost him dearly on every level, but his willingness to follow the example of Jesus in forgiving led him into a ministry of peace among some of the most hardened terrorists of our time.

As a child I once met Pastor Tokhio Matsumato, the Headmaster of the girls' school in Hiroshima, out of which only he and three pupils survived the atom bomb; who found the grace to travel the world preaching forgiveness. I met him when I was ten years old, but I've never forgotten the man's outrageous grace in forgiving those who dropped an A bomb on his school. This was forgiveness against the odds.

Forgiveness is not an instantaneous one-off act. It's a day-on-day and year-on-year work of redemption. If we will let Him, Christ can take our wounds, our prejudices, our hurts, our arrogant pride, our suspicions of others, our dark shadows of intolerance, and exchange them for the grace to live transformed and transforming lives.

We can look towards a world of societal meltdown, with terrorism, violence and aggression at the core; or we can look towards a society rich in the cultures and experiences of its citizens: a society where love, grace and harmony characterise and motivate our daily contact, a society which reflects the very nature of the kingdom of heaven – for in Christ there is no East or West.

If we are to see a society that is integrated, fair, equal and free, we must be prepared to work for it. Christians must not become too concerned with their own church politics to reach out to those of other cultures and faiths. This is the work of God, and through His redeeming love we really can change the future.

This journey towards peace and harmony begins when we pull down the ugly walls of partition which separate us, clouding our thinking and impairing our judgment. In the New Testament, the apostle James wrote: 'What causes wars, and what causes fightings among you? Is it not your passions that are at war in your members?' (James 4:1, RSV).

Love is always the best choice. Sometimes it's not easy to see the way ahead. But one thing's for sure: in all of our dealings with others we are called to be loving, and love must be the key to how we live and work, a love which doesn't come from us, but is drawn from the heart of our heavenly Father, whose love knows no limit.

Discussion Questions

1 'Birds of a feather flock together.' Why is it so much easier to 'stick with our own kind'? What do we gain, and what do we lose in doing so?

2 The Bible teaches 'Here there is no Greek or Jew, circumcised or uncircumcised, barbarian, Scythian, slave or free, but Christ is all, and is in all' (Colossians 3:11), offering an aspirational model for a community where people of all cultures are respected. To what extent do you think we are really living this aspect of our faith? How, in practical terms, might we extend this vision for the church into wider society? How might we respect the religious traditions and freedom of others while upholding the distinctiveness of our own?

3 A review by Sir Derek Wanless, former chief executive of a leading UK bank, has revealed that black children are five times less likely to be registered as 'gifted and talented' than white children, and three times more likely to be excluded from school. How might we work towards a fairer world for our youngest citizens?

4 Twenty per cent of those who are in jail in the UK come from an ethnic minority community – whilst they make up only 8 per cent of the population. How do you think this discrepancy can have come about?

5 The Foreign Policy Centre report found that those 'who are made to wait indefinitely, who are given little information or who are treated disrespectfully will clearly be less willing to adapt and cooperate with the integration process.' 'When an alien lives with you in your land, do not ill-treat him. The alien living with you must be treated as one of your native-born. Love him as yourself, for you were aliens in Egypt. I am the Lord your God' (Leviticus 19:33). How might we create sensible limits to immigration, and keep in place appropriate monitoring of our borders and population, while at the same time considering the plight of asylum seekers with compassion?

6 Peter Riddell of the Department of Islamic Studies at the London School of Theology wonders if the concept of multiculturalism has been based on flawed thinking. Archbishop John Sentamu has said: 'Multiculturalism has seemed to imply, wrongly for me, that we should let other cultures express themselves without letting the majority culture tell us about its glories, its struggles, its joys, and its pains.' What is your response to these observations?

7 In the creation stories of Genesis 1 and 2 we see that human dignity stems from the concept that we are created in the image of God. Because of this, all human beings are worthy of respect regardless of their abilities, status, race or gender. How might we carry forward this understanding in the kind of society we are working to create?

8 The apostle James wrote: 'What causes wars, and what causes fightings among you? Is it not your passions that are at war in your members?' What attitudes and experiences do you think lie at the roots of racism and racist behaviour?

Chapter Four

Doing the Right Thing in a Sex-Mad Society

Sex and the media

We are a society preoccupied with sex.

A quick glance through a typical week's TV listings reveals a whole raft of programmes which are dominated by sex.

Programmes which would once have been classified as 'pornographic' are now trailed enthusiastically in the quality press.

On *Temptation Island* a fly on the wall TV crew watches as couples in long-term relationships offer all their domestic happiness as the stake in a sexual game of risk. They are separated from each other and then tempted to become sexually and emotionally involved with someone else in an idyllic romantic setting.

Footage of their sexual encounters is then shown to their partners while the television audience watches the unfolding heartbreak in voyeuristic fascination. This bizarre form of entertainment desecrates and offends even the most basic human understanding of commitment and fidelity, confusing fantasy with reality in its failure to acknowledge that what we have seen is not a momentary scene from a passage of fiction but the beginning of the unravelling of entire lives. The damage done by such betrayals is not ephemeral but permanent.

In *Ibiza Uncovered* we follow the adventures of a party of young Brits through a high-spirited and alcohol-sodden week of hedonism, in which the main criterion for a good time is the number of people they've slept with. Those who emerge as the heroes of the series are the ones who make the greatest number of sexual conquests in the course of their time away.

Meanwhile, Jerry Springer continues to televise his horrific exposés of the tangle of human relationships. The 'I'm sleeping with my half-sister whilst engaged to my cousin and having an affair with the man who was supposed to be giving me away' type scenario leads to an understanding of human sexuality that has no room for the fulfilment of faithfulness, companionship, and the quiet peace of real trust.

Some of the programmes go even further. In *Hotter Sex*, Sky One 'sexperts' brief three couples in ways to improve their sex lives. As if that's not enough, the heat sensory cameras follow them into the bedroom where they proceed to try out the new techniques.

According to a *Times* TV review of this series, Deborah and Dave found that their friendship was undermining their capacity for unadulterated lust – but this was nothing that a PVC catsuit couldn't cure!

Meanwhile, Channel 4 has been screening *Sex tips for girls*. The mind boggles at what some people are willing to say and do in front of an invisible audience numbered in millions. The main advice for women in one episode was to undergo a Taoist course in 'vaginal breathing' with the ultimate goal of achieving a 'full body orgasm'!

In a meeting with one of the heads of acquisitions at a major satellite broadcasting channel, I asked him why his channel was screening so much of this immoral and pornographic trash. 'It's very simple,' he replied, 'it pulls in the ratings, and in my business ratings are everything!' In a more and more competitive market for audience share the broadcasters have come to rely on the effective drawing power of sexually explicit material.

What we are seeing on our TV screens is a symptom of a

much more serious malaise. The most urgent moral issue isn't 'should pornography be more strictly censored?' but a more fundamental question about the meaning of sex in contemporary society and its value in human relationships.

If sex is just an appetite to be satisfied, like physical hunger, then it's little wonder that sexually explicit TV programmes are so popular. In a society which considers that sex is only to be exploited for personal pleasure, it follows that men and women will come to view each other as nothing more than sex objects. As a result, many individuals will simply use others for their own sexual satisfaction. The result is a society immensely impoverished, missing out on the richness of fulfilment that can only come with faithful intimacy and real trust.

Christians who take the teaching of the Bible and the Church seriously find in sexual encounter a precious and sacred dimension – for sex is God's good gift, the joyous expression of trustworthy, committed, honest love that is in it for the long haul. The Christian understanding is that sex satisfies not only our physical hunger and one of our basic human needs, but also our yearning to belong, to be understood, to be really loved. Without tenderness, faithfulness and real self-giving, sexual encounter is ultimately unsatisfying and incomplete. The Bible teaches that sex is not just a quick grope and fumble, a brief sensation to satisfy an instinct as inconsequential as scratching an itch; it is, at the profoundest level, becoming one – whether we realise and intend that, or not.

Some Christians want to turn the clock back, to reinstate Victorian moral standards and press for greater legal safeguards and powers of censorship over the propagators of these erotic words and images; but there would be no public appetite for censorious moralising or a gospel of negativity.

The most urgent task is that we engage our community in a new debate about the true meaning of sexuality and press the case for revaluing sex within our culture. We must persuade the rising generation that if sex has become meaningless, we have lost the highest expression of human love. In a world that knows all too well the devastation caused by the AIDS virus and the wreckage in the aftermath of divorce, we may find a readier audience than we expected.

Censored!

For many years a friend of mine worked in the photographic department of a major tabloid newspaper. The technicians in his department spent much of their time perfecting the nude pin-ups which the paper featured every day.

It's hardly surprising that their off duty seating area faced a wall plastered with erotic pictures of young women. My friend, a Baptist deacon, found the pictures on the wall offensive and distasteful. As he was the shop steward of the photographic department he asked if the pictures could be removed because he objected to spending his lunch breaks in front of this constantly changing display of pornographic images.

His proposal to remove the pictures met with fierce resistance. Relationships in the department grew more and more strained, so my friend withdrew his opposition to the display, and simply asked his church to pray about the situation.

Soon afterwards the management decided to restructure the workspace, and this led to the photos being taken down and the wall being demolished. The workers couldn't find a new space in which to place their nude pictures, so the issue was dropped. It was one of the strangest answers to prayer that I've ever encountered, and demonstrates that such situations can sometimes be challenged directly in the heavenly realm, the real location of the battle, without creating unproductive antagonism and confrontation.

The display of pornographic magazines on newsagents bookshelves raises similar issues. Recently the Member of Parliament for Cosby, Claire Curtis-Thomas, took a Bill to the British Parliament to regulate the sale of such magazines.

The MP stated that she found it bewildering that children could 'legally and freely' access such sexually explicit magazines, and called for an independent body to regulate the sale of such publications.

She suggested that such magazines should be kept on the top shelf of newsagents' display stands with the understanding that they should always be covered and wrapped. She pointed out that though it would be illegal for her to quote their 'graphic and repulsive' content in the House of Commons, the nation's children could look at them and buy them without restraint!

The MP argued that 'whilst freedom of speech and expression are rightly defended foundations of our society, it is frankly disgusting that these liberties can be exploited to the extent where children have free access to such degrading explicit material.'

The organization called Truth about Rape supported the Bill. They felt that women were sordidly devalued in 'lads' magazines, and often portrayed as cheap sex objects. There is no statistical evidence to prove a direct link between pornography and rape, but this pressure-group believes that pornography creates a culture in which women are de-valued and demeaned and are therefore more likely to be sexually abused. At the time of writing Claire's campaign is ongoing.

Pornographic exploitation, whether of women, children or men, is no longer confined to back-street sex shops, Soho porn cinemas or mail order magazines. Pornography is now a multi-billion-dollar global industry. The growth of satellite TV with its multiplicity of porn channels, which cater for every kind of sexual taste; the opening up of the internet with its plethora of porn sites; the development of erotic phone services; the appearance of highly sexualised computer games; and the widespread distribution of pornographic

DVDs mean that sexually explicit material has now permeated every gateway into the mainstream mass market. Research from agencies such as Care indicates that addiction to these explicit images is growing and that many Christians are included among the customers and voyeurs in the mega-industry that pornography has become. Government control seems ineffective in curbing the tide, and the limited resources of public funding to manage the situation are mainly used to monitor paedophile and masochistic outlets.

Society's view of sex has been cheapened and devalued into a thrills-for-sale commodity – a procession of images and encounters whose purpose is to arouse and which carry no meaning beyond immediate pleasure. A very large proportion of our society seems to have lost its basic understanding of what God intended sex to be, and has drifted toward voyeurism, self-gratification, and lust. Tighter censorship no longer answers the situation. These pornographic images are now so pervasive and the means of access to them so prolific that controlling is no longer a realistic option.

If we want our young people to be emotionally literate, thoughtful and caring human beings we must protect them from those images and ideas which are dangerous or destructive. Erotic response is healthy and good and part of a teenager's developing sexuality, but we don't want our young people exposed to perverse sexual acts or sadistic sexual practices before they have the maturity to understand how destructive such behaviour can be. Their protection begins with the example set in their home and family; but protecting them in the wider world is much easier to discuss than to achieve.

Effective censorship of this massive volume of explicit material is about as practical as King Canute ordering the tide to go out! This wave of pornography is sweeping through our society. Every effort to moderate it is evaded.

Just as soon as one channel is blocked or one lad's mag is moved to the top shelf, another ten forms of pornography appear over the horizon.

Recently, regulators monitoring the web discovered that many of the interactive sites such as 'Youtube' and 'Facebook', popular with millions of teenagers and previously thought to be harmless, were being permeated with unregulated pornography in hundreds of listings that seemed innocent and did not advertise the true nature of their content. Just as soon as the regulators clean up one web address, the floodtide of pornography wells up in another!

We must encourage the regulators to do what they can, but we need to focus our efforts on parents and educators. We must help young people to understand the inherent dangers of pornography and encourage them to take personal responsibility for censoring what they see, watch and read. We need to explain to young people that pornography can be harmful to their development as mature human beings, and encourage their self-respect, strengthening the sense of their inherently spiritual stature as human beings. We cannot rely on the sex education provided in school to take account of the wider perspective in which we so profoundly believe.

The opportunity to demonstrate by our lives that chaste, responsible sexuality supports the best relationships and the best sex surely has to be one of the biggest mission opportunities a fallen world has ever offered us!

Sex education

Several UK initiatives have been launched to address the quality of sex education in schools. Some Christian parents have felt concern about these new programmes, especially where the moral values communicated are at variance with the teaching of the Bible and the Christian tradition. These parents feel that the responsibility for sex education properly lies with the family, as the understanding of sexual relationships should be formed within the holistic framework of a value system proceeding from a whole philosophy of life.

Christian parents have reacted with particular concern to sex education programmes relying heavily on the promotion of contraception, especially where this may involve distribution of condoms or morning-after contraceptive pills to students. This concern seems to be justified at every level, since statistics indicate that wherever such a sex education method has been monitored and researched, it has actually been shown to increase, rather than reduce, the number of teenage pregnancies.

The Family Education Trust is an independent think-tank seeking to promote responsible attitudes to marriage and family life, and conducting research into the causes and effects of family breakdown. The Trust measured the number of teenage pregnancies in the areas targeted by the government's Teenage Pregnancy Unit, with its radical methods of sex education focusing and relying heavily on the promotion and provision of contraception for the prevention of teenage pregnancy and sexually transmitted disease.

The report published by the Trust in 2002, 'Sex Education or Indoctrination', claimed that sex education is being used as a 'manipulative tool to replace the influence of parents with the authority of the state'. The author of the report, Valerie Riches, a former social worker, says this form of education 'sows confusion in a child's mind about right and wrong and presents only one moral absolute – the use of condoms.'

Official figures support this Trust's argument. The pregnancy rate in Cornwall, for example, rose from 306 schoolgirl pregnancies to 359 after the radical new course had been tried out. Similar rises in teen pregnancies were recorded in Torbay (up 22 percent), Solihull (up 17 percent) and York (up 34 percent). All were areas where pupils had been given free condoms, more sex education and confidential health checks.

Professor David Paton from the University of Nottingham pinpoints one of the key elements in reducing teenage pregnancies as 'healthy relationships within the family unit'. He believes that where parents talk openly with their children about sex that there is much less likelihood of a teenage pregnancy within the family. He believes that the distribution of free condoms sends entirely the wrong message.

Unlike the UK, the United States has seen a massive movement towards sexual abstinence among young people. Organisations such as True Love Waits and the Silver Ring Thing have encouraged young people to keep their virginity until marriage. This has lead to a steady decade-long reduction in teenage pregnancies in America. This movement has been actively supported by many Christian parents and leaders in the USA.

The Revd Michael Ovey, a Christian lawyer in the UK, observes: 'Here, sex education can manifest a double tyranny: that of parents refusing responsibilities of instruction on the grounds the state will discharge them, and that of the state inculcating values of liberal secular pluralism.'

Sex education that is preoccupied with the mechanics of sex and methods of contraception, without offering responsible discussion about the meaning of sex and the best moral context for sexual relationships, is at best inadequate, at worst profoundly damaging. It is perhaps to be expected that, in the regions where condoms have been distributed so freely, young people have experimented with sexual practice rather than exercising personal restraint. *Bliss* magazine surveyed 2,000 14-year-old girls and discovered that one in five in the UK has had sex, and with an average of three partners. Half of the sexually active girls said that they had regretted the experience.

The editor of *Bliss* concluded: 'Peer pressure from their friends plays a great role in this. They are desperate not to be the last virgin in school, but often they are not emotionally mature enough to deal with the situation.' The magazine found that alcohol was a major contributory factor to sexual experimentation, with 60 percent of the girls admitting that they were drunk when they first had sexual intercourse.

Seventy percent of all the girls in the survey said they would have liked more advice; 44 percent of the girls said that they mainly relied on magazines for sexual information; and 57 percent said they had never discussed sex with their parents at all.

When preparation for a lecture required me to review a range of the teen publications such as the girls had said they relied on for guidance and information, I was shocked to discover how sexually permissive were the attitudes they encouraged.

The church has a responsibility to young people to challenge the assumptions of those who exercise such a powerful influence over them, and to question the wisdom of ethics that encourage promiscuity. In accepting sexually active teenage years too uncritically as the norm, both the teen magazines and the UK state education programme may in fact be contributing towards the creation of a norm which is not in the best interests of young people.

Bliss magazine also discovered that 65 percent of the readers who responded to the survey said they had unprotected sex, and nearly half had sexual intercourse on a casual basis in the context of a very transient relationship or passing encounter. These statistics indicate that sex in our society has become morally devalued, with young teens following the lead of the social norms presented in the classroom, on the television, on the internet and in magazines for their age group. The result is an increasing tendency to a pattern of sexual behaviour which leaves people disappointed, empty, lonely and frustrated.

Promiscuity also creates vulnerability to sexually transmitted diseases, and not surprisingly instances have risen dramatically. The incidence of gonorrhoea in the UK had more than doubled in the past decade, according to the

British Journal of Infection Control in 2004. This means that tens of thousands of young people are jeopardising their health because of a casual lifestyle driven by the anxious desire to conform.

The Chief Executive of the Family Planning Association, Ann Weyman, responded to the figures about sexually transmitted disease by saying that 'relationship education in schools should be mandatory'. Indeed it should! How could we as a society have allowed educationalists with such a careless philosophy to take control of the hearts and minds of vulnerable young teenagers? And how could those with power in government have been so blind as to permit it, without seeing the risks to health and well-being? Other figures from the *Bliss* magazine survey give a glimmer of hope: 94 percent of 14-year-old girls said that 'love and affection' were more important than sex. The survey reveals that what girls aspire to, and what happens in reality, are two very different things. The editor of *Bliss*, Lisa Smosarski, summed it up when she wrote, 'This survey shows that teenagers really are new traditionalists – they want to get married and have children, yet they are having sex earlier and often under the influence of alcohol.'

The research indicates that young people may be ready to respond to a new moral lead. In recent years, responding to concerns about heart disease and obesity, information from the government, education and the media have successfully combined to create a culture in which information and suggestions about healthy eating and active lifestyle are vigorously promoted. It seems urgently necessary to begin a parallel movement encouraging young people to self-censor what they read or watch, communicating that pornography does not enhance personal, mental, emotional and spiritual health, and that promiscuity is not a passport to fun-filled relationships, but a recipe for isolation, psychological emptiness and physical disease.

We must stand with our young people in celebrating the

true nature of sex as fulfilment through sharing a life together, not using other people as tools for masturbation. We must stand with them in questioning this insidious culture that suggests pornography to be the norm and encourage them to make informed and critical judgements about the images which they choose to see. We live in a democratic society committed to freedom of expression, and so cannot rely on censors to screen images we deem unsuitable from young eyes and minds in a society where the consensus is increasingly permissive. Nevertheless, I have every confidence that young people can find the moral resolve to seek the true meaning of sex.

We must help young people to develop the kind of good personal judgment which can protect them from harm. Effective censorship is an impossible dream; and relying on censorship in any case carries the inherent weakness of relying on the protection of another rather than on personally acquired wisdom and strength – but good education about sex is not only a real possibility but an urgent responsibility, and those of us who have influence in this field must do our utmost to make sure that it happens.

If (as seems to be the case) the provision of sex education in schools falls significantly below our standards and expectations, then it is incumbent upon Christians to supply the lack, in terms of both guidance and information. Several groups have started to work in this area, and they have found a ready response from both schools and students.

Recently I met the leaders of Challenge Teams, a group that visits schools to talk about sex. However, they do not focus on how to practise safe sex, but on why the group members personally had decided to save sex for marriage. In their first tour the teams spoke to 6,000 pupils, mostly aged 13 and 14 (years 9 and 10). The team members soon dispelled any myths that they were anti-sex, ugly or sex-starved! But then they introduced a new word – chastity.

They presented a lifestyle of chastity as not only possible, but desirable. They spoke of their own beliefs that respect for your own sexuality, and that of others, is a great way to live. They spoke of a lifestyle free from sexually transmitted infections and unwanted pregnancy, and a freedom to enjoy uncomplicated friendship with people of the opposite sex, saving the special gift of sexual union for the 'Mr/Miss Right' that they would one day want to marry.

Reading the responses to the Challenge presentation from both students and teachers, I am convinced that this group is pioneering a way which many other groups should attempt to follow. I was particularly moved by the comment of one Year 10 Head, who wrote: 'Personally I do not particularly agree with their message but it was put over in a very persuasive way without any "geek" angle that the kids would have picked up on. If you could contact the school next autumn we would like to book them again.'

We have shown far too much reticence in advocating a Christian moral perspective about sex. The vast majority of 14-year-olds are looking for a lifestyle that can make them happy and is worth their respect, but they need to be given the right kind of role models to emulate and the right kind of ideals to reach for. Too often Christians think that the battle is lost, when in fact in the debate about the meaning of sex, our time is now. It's a debate in which we have a crucial contribution to make.

Another group, known as the Silver Ring Thing, is gradually gaining ground. It is a movement in which young people make a pledge of chastity to God, and wear a silver ring as a public witness to their inner commitment.

I have met quite a number of young people who have made this kind of commitment. I am convinced that their witness to a lifestyle of personal chastity is strategic in influencing their peers. Some of them spoke to me of the kind of ridicule they have endured at school from both fellow students and staff; but they also spoke of the way that many of their friends appreciated their willingness to point to a more radical lifestyle and a more mature view of life. We should applaud this kind of initiative and clearly stand with those who are willing to make responsible life choices, and to follow Christ.

The meaning of sex

One of the most profound plays I have seen in a long time premiered at the Donmar Warehouse in London in 1998. It's a play about sex, but it's not erotic or sensuous, just very, very sad.

Sleeping Around is a collaboration by four of the sharpest new playwrights from England, Ireland, Scotland and Wales (Hilary Fannin, Stephen Greenhorn, Abi Morgan, and Mark Ravenhill). A multitude of scenes of likely and unlikely sexual connection depict extraordinary moments in ordinary lives. The theatre was packed with people in their twenties, and the roars of laughter and thunderous applause spoke of an emotional identification with what was being portrayed. It was a review of the role of sex in contemporary society. These scenarios depict how sex in Britain is often about anything except the expression of tender love in a permanent marital relationship.

There was the scene between the powerful female sales executive and the scientist she wants to seduce. He will be useful to her in her career – the powerful woman, and the weak man she wants to manipulate. Sex, in the game of sexual politics between men and women.

Then came the dowdy university professor and the admiring student who means nothing to him. She is vulnerable and weak, hanging on to his every word and offering him sex so that, just for a moment, he might show some interest in her. Sex, in the abuse of the weak and desperate.

And the lonely woman who can't sleep, trying to seduce the attendant at the till in the all-night petrol station. They are separated by thick vandal-proof glass. He is locked in by a security timer and they are both recorded by surveillance cameras. She is desperate for someone to love her, to hold her and to care for her. He just wants to read his comic. A tragic tale of lonely disconnected people in a world which insulates them from each other. Sex, seen as a desperate cure for loneliness, for isolation and for personal pain.

Then there was the married couple who are sharing a hotel room with thin walls. He has been drinking, and she wants nothing more to do with him. They are facing the breakdown of their relationship and their inability to express any affection to each other. Their long silences are accompanied by the screams of sexual passion from the room next door. Sex in failure, in defeat, in brokenness.

And the first date, with two young students, shy and embarrassed, trying to communicate their love for each other, but each somehow unable to interpret what the other is saying. Distant, reserved, hardly daring to touch. Sex in the naivety of the first flush of love.

Then there were the two hurried lovers on a park bench. She, cheating on her husband, and he, late for a business appointment in Brighton. Her passion, punctuated by his frequent glances at his watch. At last, in desperation, she snatches it from him and changes the time. She is trying to tell him that what she feels for him can't be measured in minutes, but is somehow eternal. And he is trying to find out if he's missed his appointment. Sex in the rush of life, and the unsatisfied hunger for something richer, deeper and more lasting.

And the deeply touching scene of the air hostess who is sunbathing at the hotel pool on her regular stop-over from New York. She's seen it all – slept with them all – yet, somehow, remains deeply unsatisfied. The captain she loves is unobtainable and beyond her reach, and beside her at the pool lies the young man with AIDS wondering what he has given his life for. A quick moment of passion with a stranger.

Sex in the broken lives of people who have never been fulfilled. Sex as tragedy.

There were many other scenes, too. About the cheapness of sex today, its transience, its unimportance and its pain. What a distance between what God intended sex to be and what our society has made it.

The play was at times hilariously funny and then painfully sad. Most of all, I felt the affirmation of what I already believed: that sex outside a deep, loving relationship is not what God planned. Our promiscuous society is using sex for other purposes, and is reaping a harvest of pain.

In the last scene, a young female executive is looking up at the moon, and the Cola symbol her company has projected on to it by laser, a symbol of the tawdriness of consumer society desecrating the beauty of creation with the cheap toys of technology. She cries out in anguish, 'When I was young all I wanted was someone to hold me, to care for me, to love me for who I really am, someone I could really be one with.'

The heart cry is there in each of us. Sex does have a part to play in the rich relationships between men and women. It is part of God's redemptive purpose for us. Where have we gone wrong?

Christians recognise that the cornerstone of the universe is the relationship between Father, Son and Holy Spirit. It's a relationship of perfect love, perfect unity and separate identity. This relationship is at the very heart of Christianity. It's a relationship which existed before the planet, and which will outlast history. It's the true model for all human relationships. Christians cannot deny the importance of rich relationships without denying the character of God Himself. God gave sex for lasting loving relationships epitomised by the kind of commitment at the heart of Christian marriage. Taken out of a faithful and loving context such as this, sex quickly loses its importance and its value.

Transient relationships and short periods of cohabitation, aren't what God intended sex for. Alice Westgate, a thirty-one-year-old single journalist writing recently in the *Daily Mail* about her three experiences of cohabitation, concluded: 'You never quite commit that last little but of yourself – the reasons for being together are more to do with habit than conviction – and at the end you're left with no recognition that you spent a serious amount of time being seriously close to another person.'

As this experience is replicated across a whole generation, what does it really mean in human terms? What will it mean for the children born into such relationships? Reviewing the 'baby-boomer' generation of the 1960s and 1970s, Richard Peace, a professor at Fuller Theological Seminary, noted that:

> In striving to redefine relationships Boomers shattered the so-called traditional family. They promoted promiscuity, which in turn sparked an epidemic of sexually transmitted diseases – herpes, Chlamydia and AIDS. They divorced each other at a headlong, reckless pace. They delayed childbearing and aborted unborn children in record numbers.

He believes that the generation of the 1980s are still reeling from all this. They see themselves as the victims of a so-called relational revolution. Professor Peace's outspoken views are supported by other more recent research, indicating that children from broken families are more likely to replicate the experience in their own families.

A recent study conducted by Kathleen Kiernan at the London School of Economics shows that parental divorce has lasting and profound effects on children's emotional development and their ability to form lasting relationships. Four out of ten men and women whose parents split up when they were children had seen their first marriage or co-habitation break down by the time they were 33 – 10 per cent more than those whose parents had stayed together. The report concluded that broken relationships can adversely affect the children involved. Significantly, women from divorced families are nearly twice as likely to become teenage mothers as those who grew up with both parents.

This happens because the family, which should be an enclosure for safety, often becomes an emotional kick-boxing ring. Not only are there insufficient boundaries against external threats, but the parents themselves are often the threat.

Where children grow up in an unstable background they often don't feel safe and secure. They suffer from a diminished sense of individual identity and definition, and in some cases the child's personality has been so distorted by past experiences that the disorder becomes integral to them.

In a disturbing article in the *New Statesman*, John Lloyd noted that 'The rearing of children must be reinvented because ... stable families, even if they continue to be the largest element in the rearing of children, will not again monopolise the scene.'

The central relationships of the nuclear family, forged between husbands and wives and parents and children, are under great threat. I am convinced that Christians have a vital contribution to make in resisting this social trend, and much to say in the national debate about the future of family life.

God gave sex to be an integral part of deep and lasting relationships. Some people are called to singleness, happy with their own company, celibate by choice and vocation, whether in community with others or as solitaries set apart. But the majority of people are lonely living without a partner and flourish best when they belong to another person in a beautiful lasting relationship. Sex as part of such a relationship is a means of expressing our incalculable value as human beings, a special and precious blessing of loving and being loved.

Transient, short-term relationships may be a norm for our society today, but they are not God's best way. That's why Christians need to model the value of lasting relationships as the central building block of society. Stability, community and fidelity nourish the soul.

Ephemeral relationships, or relationship breakdown, are also consuming of emotional and spiritual resources. It is impossible to give very generously of time, attention and energy at the same time as rebuilding a torn life and broken household, or while switch-backing on the roller-coaster ride of one new relationship after another. Human beings are social creatures, and Christians are called to offer love and support in community. Transient relationships create the double negative of a life that not only has nothing left over from relational turmoil to offer stable and steady support to others, but also tends to require support from those households characterised by faithful, stable, abiding relationships.

Paul urged the people at Corinth to 'avoid sexual immorality. Any other sin a man commits does not affect his body; but the man who is guilty of sexual immorality sins against his own body. Don't you know that your body is the temple of the Holy Spirit who lives in you and who was given to you by God?' (1 Corinthians 6:18, 19, TEV).

Strong words indeed; and, in a sex mad society, words which challenge Christians to a lifestyle which is counter-cultural and questions the trends of popular opinion. Such a lifestyle sees sex as a gift from God for marriage: something bringing value to human relationship; never destructive to us, or abusive to those around us.

'Love is patient, love is kind ... it is not self-seeking ... does not delight in evil but rejoices with the truth. It always protects, always trusts, always hopes, always perseveres' (1 Corinthians 13:4–7). This is the ideal of Christian love; the choice to walk in the way of Christ means that the ordinary love between man and woman is blessed and overshone by the divine dimension that we call eternal life.

Great sex!

Those whose mental image of Christian marriage is reminiscent of a grim-faced Victorian couple sewn into their underwear for the long cold winter of life in church, will not have glanced through the pages of *Let's Make Love* by Jack Dominian. In this profound book Dominian, a leading Christian psychiatrist, points out that Christianity has a history of hostility to eroticism and sex. Instead of rejoicing unashamedly in sexuality as portrayed in the Song of Songs, Christians have retreated into spiritualised metaphor, or ignored the playfulness and pleasure of sex, reducing it to the functional biology of procreation.

Dominian is not suggesting, as some have accused him of doing, that we worship sexuality, but rather that we celebrate it and appreciate in this intimate connection the loving presence of the divine mystery. Dominian teaches that we should appreciate sexuality as a powerful component of the love that is the heartbeat and essence of God.

Though the world has gone mad in its obsession with sex and sexuality, the Christian tradition has at times rejected the beauty and joy of sex – making it into a thing that's somehow unmentionable or dirty. The Christian faith is a celebration of Christ's incarnation – the Word becoming flesh – and so is all about opening the way in to allow the divine mystery to shine in and through the ordinary physical details of our lives. When we say God is love, but forget to acknowledge the occasions we experience sexual love as God-appointed moments, we are leaving the power of the gospel, its incarnational wisdom, untapped.

The people who feature in the television programmes *Temptation Island*, *Ibiza Uncovered*, *The Springer Show*, *Hotter Sex* and *Sex Tips for Girls*, have chosen a very sensual interpretation of what sex can be, within a very narrow physical definition. It would be understandable for them to mistake the Christian view, emphasising as it does the sacred trust of sexual relationship and the importance of chastity, as that of kill-joys who have no idea how good sex can be.

Perhaps it's time we went public about our appreciation of sex and our enjoyment of it! Indeed, perhaps it's time we made it clear that, in the context of Christian marriage, sex can be so satisfying, offering fulfilment beyond imagining, exactly because it is so much more than a cheap thrill. It's part of our affirmation of identity, it's integral to our growth as individuals, it's part of the process of healing which comforts us in the knocks of life, it's a place of reconciliation and a joyous expression of thanksgiving. Sex is one of the supreme affirmations of our humanity.

The sex-therapy shows on TV point to the ultimate vision of sexual pleasure as the 'full body orgasm', and imply that once you've got this you've got the ultimate sexual experience. You've experienced *life's* ultimate climax.

This is a really sad view of sexuality. If the ultimate sexual experience really is thought to be a five star orgasm, then it is the sex therapists setting that limit on our aspirations who haven't lived! I believe that good sex is about making love, which encompasses so very much more than making orgasms. Sexual dysfunction makes people unhappy, and sexual ineptitude can create frustration: certainly sexual counselling and therapy have their place. Although promiscuity and pornography do not bless society, increased information about sex has been very liberating, doing much to dispel fear about bodily processes, and ignorance about simple sexual mechanics. This liberation has been especially helpful to women, for whom the process of sexual arousal and physical fulfilment is not always straightforward. Indeed we are not all soul – getting the physical part of our sexual relationships right is important – but the physical dimension of sex will never satisfy by itself, because it's not full body orgasms that people need so much as body-mind-and-spirit orgasms. It is the engagement of the whole being that generates the wonderful afterglow of peace when two people who really love each other with complete understanding and commitment lie contented in each other's arms.

As Dominian concludes: 'Although orgasm is clearly the ultimate goal of intercourse, in my opinion it's not i sultimate meaning. Sexual intercourse is an encounter between persons and its ultimate meaning is interpersonal...This is a communication of love. It is a language that shifts the individual from egoism to a mutuality of sharing. They are sharing each other. It is a language that shifts the technology of pleasure to mutual commitment. And finally, it is a shift from potentially meaningless pleasure to meaningful interaction.'

Any view of sex which is no more than hedonistic, self-centred, casual encounter is so reductionist as to be degrading. The television programmes that purport to be journalism or a portrayal of reality, but are really just pornography for voyeurs with empty lives, make sex look not exciting but just sordid. It is those who see sex as an expression of love in the context of a lifelong relationship who have really lived and really loved. In this context sex transcends the physical and becomes a spiritual celebration of the reality of God's love.

In the 1930s Renee Spitz and John Bowlby, studying the cause of infant deaths in foundling homes, observed that even when adequately fed, and kept clean, warm and protected from disease, a baby is likely to die without cuddles and love.

Human beings crave the nourishment of intimacy, affection and companionship. Whether people are celibate and single, married and faithful, randy youngsters on the make, prostitutes with full lists of clients, or Don Juan veterans of many conquests, still they will not be happy until they know themselves loved. If they are not happy, their sexual encounters will not be happy either.

The good news of the Christian gospel, that we are loved for ourselves unconditionally and just as we are, will not only be the salvation of our souls, but incidentally open up the possibility of the hottest sex the human body can stand.

Discussion Questions

1 To what extent is the preoccupation with sex evident in the media a fair reflection of the interests and preferences of your family and friends?

2 What balance can we find between supplying customer demand for sexually explicit material in the newsagent, and protecting the innocence of children who also shop there?

3 Many teenagers rely on magazines published for their age group for information about sex. How do you think teen magazines might responsibly guide and inform their readers?

4 Which kinds of sex education seem to you to be the most valuable? What are your thoughts about making contraceptives available to teenagers through programmes of sex education?

5 What role did your parents play in your sex education? What should the balance of responsibility be, between home and school, in the education of children about sex?

6 'Teenagers really are ... traditionalists – they want to get married and have children, yet they are having sex earlier and often under the influence of alcohol' (Lisa Smosarski, Editor of *Bliss* magazine). What can be done to support teenagers' need for stability and real relationships in the face of so much cultural pressure to experiment sexually?

7 What do you think of Challenge Teams and The Silver Ring Thing? How might their message be offered to your neighbourhood, church or school?

8 'Don't you know that your body is the temple of the Holy Spirit who lives in you and who was given to you by God?' (1 Corinthians 6:19, TEV). What are the best ways to combine personal holiness with a whole-hearted enthusiasm for God's gift of our sexuality?

9 'Although orgasm is clearly the ultimate goal of intercourse, in my opinion it's not its ultimate meaning' (Jack Dominian). How might we find a wise balance between the spiritual and

the physical aspects of sex? How can we encourage Christian people to be adequately and imaginatively informed without encouraging voyeurism or a mechanistic understanding of making love?

10 Some Christians believe any contraception is wrong because God intended sex for procreation. Some believe that sex is primarily about personal encounter, and family planning is a separate issue. What do you think is God's purpose for sex?

Chapter Five

Doing the Right Thing in the Media

Whenever I pick up the TV remote I know that I can instantly access television programming which includes everything from wall-to-wall movies, food programmes, chat shows, variety programmes, sit-coms, soaps, news bulletins, game shows and porn channels.

This ever increasing array of digital and satellite channels has given me more and more choice – but with it has come a plethora of unanswered questions.

Do I have the maturity to make the right decisions about what I choose to watch? Are there enough governmental controls over what's being shown? Is more exposure to this multiplicity of media outlets doing me good or doing me harm? Does more choice actually produce better television? And how do I know how to 'do the right thing' in choosing what to watch whenever I surf the massive array of channels available to me?

If I don't have an understanding of the power of the media over me, or a sense of the responsibility that I must exercise over it, how can I really live as Christ would want me to live?

The news

My own '15 minutes of fame' occurred in February 2006. My mobile rang at about 10 am, and subsequently my office and home phones all started to ring too. Some invisible network was spreading my numbers around, and I've never under-stood quite how it worked.

I had done the last media interview with Norman Kember, the Christian peace activist, before his visit to Iraq and his subsequent kidnap ordeal. My interview with him became more significant than either of us had ever imagined and was broadcast on many of the main news channels, from BBC One's 10 pm TV news slot through to repeated airings on Al Jazeera, the Arabic news network.

The news of Norman Kember's release through a military operation led by the SAS, and the (false) accusation that he had refused to say thank-you to the troops who rescued him, made this a 'top of the hour' news story.

I spent much of the following two days travelling from studio to studio in the chauffeur driven limousines which the news teams sent to my door. It was a revelation. I began to realise just how much 'the news' has become a production line industry.

As I sat in the studio waiting to do Radio 4's *World at One*, the researcher from BBC News 24 was hovering to whisk me away to a TV studio several floors above. This interview was repeated for hours afterwards.

No sooner had I arrived there then I was hurried down the long grey corridors of the BBC's White City complex to the studios of BBC World Television. Then on into Central London by car to the BBC World Service studios at Aldwych where I was pitched into a fierce debate with some pro-military philosophy lecturer who was sitting in a studio in Lancaster, and then on to the make-up room at ITN.

Here at Channel 4 News I was 'powdered' alongside Jon Snow before a live grilling on the main news programme of the evening. I was somewhat reassured when Jon Snow had promised in make-up that he'd give me an easy ride, but my confidence evaporated when the live broadcast started, the robotic cameras moved towards me, and he swivelled his chair round to face me and asked:

'Where was God when Kember was kidnapped?'

My heart raced. 'As always, He was right by his side,' I replied. Snow smirked.

As I was rushing from studio to studio there were phone interviews with national and local radio stations too numerous to list. Whilst travelling home on the train after the last interview (the limos had all suddenly vanished) I was called by the duty producer at BBC News 24 inviting me to join Peter Sissons for a four-hour news special entitled 'Kember returns' the following day.

That Saturday afternoon, over a prolonged live broadcast, with television units in Iraq, on the roof at Heathrow, in the arrivals lounge, outside Kember's home and in a helicopter hovering over his back garden, I was able to see how 'live news' is really put together. Beneath the desk a printer constantly spewed out scripts while potential questions flashed on the screens before us, and a constant maelstrom of chatter from the director's gallery filled our ears. Whenever the red light went off, Sissons would turn and ask, 'Any ideas what we could talk about next?'

This is the contemporary news environment. It is being created as we watch. No time to think, or plan, or weigh up the alternatives: only the constant drive to beat the competition in getting the latest breaking story on the screen.

I watch the news differently now. It has lost some of its mystique and much of its authority for me. It is as though I've been backstage at some glamorous West End musical and seen how the special effects were done; or been privy to the manager's instructions at half time during the Cup Final and overheard the team's strategy.

Now I see that news is entertainment. Now I understand that unless the quickly moving TV images or radio soundbites are really tantalising, the news team know that I'll surf away to other channels. Some invisible editor is selecting what is news and what isn't and their decision is based more on what pulls in a crowd than on what is of lasting significance.

What is this constant news-stream doing to me, and how is it shaping my world? Whilst countless hours are spent on the story of Madonna adopting an African child, the really significant impact of AIDS on the continent of Africa rarely gets a mention. In a contest between celebrity and poverty, celebrity wins hands down every time.

My moment of fame on the news channels has forced me to ask myself some painful questions. How has my view of the world been shaped by this ratings-driven agenda? Has my perspective been warped by a news industry which focuses more on titillation than on significance? And has my understanding of world issues lost perspective because news bulletins give so much time to issues in my own backyard?

Having seen my own contribution to the 'Kember Release' story edited, topped and tailed, mis-reported and used in packaged sound-bites, I can now see why so many celebrities refuse to be interviewed at all.

When I spoke into the reporter's microphone I was offering my words into the ether to be chopped and cut at the whim of someone I would never meet, and whose ratings-driven agenda is determined by criteria far different from my own.

Tracking back over my experience of Norman Kember's release, I would be fascinated to discover who really first said that Norman Kember did not thank the soldiers who rescued him.

If, as Norman clearly stated, he did thank the soldiers that he met, was this story the figment of someone's imagination, a mis-understanding or mis-hearing of his words – or an attempt by some night editor to create a more entertaining headline?

This aspect of the story gave the media a field day of interview opportunities. Suddenly, high-ranking generals, cabinet ministers, and Iraqi war correspondents were wheeled out to condemn Norman for his lack of gratitude without ever realising that this story was without foundation.

No matter how Norman Kember tried to put matters right, to correct the balance, or to defend his good name when he returned to London, it was too late. The damage was done. His 'ingratitude' had become a front page banner headline in the *Daily Mail*. The myth was lodged in the public psyche for ever.

I find that now, when I watch the news, disturbing questions run through my mind. What is the truth in this situation? Who really said what? Is this interview fair? Where is the balance in the content? Is there another agenda running here?

I have learned also to be especially cautious and sceptical when an evangelical Christian is 'in the frame'. The outlook on life of Bible-believing Christians is in no way in step with the spirit of the age. Because they do not conform to popular thinking, especially on issues of personal morality, they are often lampooned or presented so as to appear bigoted, prejudiced or behind the times, or as fundamentalist militants and extremists. Those evangelical Christians who don't fit the stereotype and who aren't easy to parody simply don't get air-time.

Don Horrocks, the political and social affairs commentator from the Evangelical Alliance, was recently seriously misquoted in the national press. He did an interview with a live national TV news channel to put his misrepresented comments right, and he specifically stated before the interview that he would not talk about the statement which had been so badly mis-reported.

The first few questions were serious, considered, and sensitive. But then the interviewer focused on what Don had specifically refused to talk about. The interviewer broke his agreement and, in the end, in desperation, Don felt that he had no option but to end the interview. Don could only conclude that the station was not interested in the serious issue at stake, but only in making a sensation out of something which he had never said in the first place.

It is not only evangelical Christians who are stereotyped. Sometimes it can be politicians, those representing unpopular pressure groups or those who don't stand for the majority view. Skilled interviewers, sharp tape editors and slick vision mixers have the power to make any of us look stupid. However quick witted you are, they can make you into a pathetic stereotype which is far from the real you.

This was even more painfully brought home to me when a leading Christian magazine publicly chastised me for doing something which I had not done. No-one had taken the trouble to discover if the facts were true before going to print, let alone taking the biblical injunction to seek to correct a brother privately first. It was a deeply hurtful experience, and one which unnecessarily damaged my reputation.

If I really am going to 'do the right thing' I must try to check that I'm basing my opinions on truth rather than on myth. I must make sure that I am believing the best about people, rather than scurrilous scandal which is based on nothing more than hearsay.

I am ashamed to recognise that sometimes sordid revelations about people's private lives make me feel smug, superior and judgmental, when these are hardly Christian attributes!

For over eleven years I have produced and presented a news-driven Christian programme on Premier Radio every Sunday morning. It has been a fascinating experience, and has put me on a sharp learning curve as I have attempted to engage with the world's agenda from a Christian perspective every week.

From the outset I was helped by a retired television executive called Howard Ross, the one-time producer of a weekly current affairs television show which drew an audience of millions.

He taught me that conflict draws an audience, that disagreement is interesting and that strongly held views from different perspectives make good entertainment. He also taught me that balance and fairness are a crucial part of the mix. If an interviewee leaves feeling that they have been misrepresented and misunderstood, then they are unlikely to help you again. He helped me to understand that the audience is perceptive enough to see through conflicts which have been artificially created or hyped up just to fill a gap.

I'm so grateful to Howard for his ongoing tuition about the 'art of conflict', and even more for what he taught me about integrity in media production. Where conflict is whipped up, you don't convince yourself, let alone the audience.

In a conflict-driven news industry one could be excused for thinking that agreement, unity and understanding are absent from human society. In some programmes one could imagine that kindness, consideration and an attempt to meet the other person half-way are values the human race has forgotten.

In the world of television current affairs it seems as if disagreement, accusation and argument are what make the world go round. Could it be that what makes 'good television' is, in effect, moulding a society which values conflict above reconciliation, or division over unity?

Could it be that television's never-ending drive to entertain us has led to the political dependency on spin doctors to maintain our interest? Are politicians using the news industry simply as a means of winning high scores in opinion polls? Are news channels more interested in ratings than in truth?

Could it be that the incessant quest to capture a newsworthy sound-bite has warped journalistic standards? In a world in which politicians are coached in how to evade difficult questions and how to communicate positive messages in the midst of a 'bad' news story, has 'news' actually become nothing more than propaganda?

Even in my own limited experience of interviewing cabinet ministers I have discovered just how difficult it is to get them 'off script' and talking about the moral and ethical issues which are really newsworthy. Given that millions of people honestly believe that the news reports they see are to be trusted, those of us in Christian leadership must accept responsibility to encourage Christians everywhere in the art of asking shrewd and searching questions, and going back again and again to the New Testament for a reality check in the development of our habits of mind.

I find myself becoming more and more cynical about the 'news'. Who is creating this news agenda and who decides what deserves to be the top story?

For an event to be defined as national news in the first place, it must have some characteristic that will arrest our attention; either because it concerns the life of a celebrity we immediately recognise, or brings information of a threat or disaster of sufficient magnitude to be reported, or is in some way amazing and quite out of the ordinary.

Sometimes the media will celebrate an act of heroism or great achievement – winning an Olympic medal is very newsworthy! But the most reliable material is that which will generate anxiety – 'Should we be worried about this? Will it get worse? How much is it likely to spread?'

Yet it is disconcerting to see how much of the headline-grabbing material amounts to nothing more than trivia of no real importance to anyone, while weighty matters of real social and political importance languish on the margins in the alternative press.

As Christians, we must remember to keep asking ourselves: 'What is on God's heart and what should be on mine? In following the prompting of news agendas, am I allowing myself to be distracted from the biblical agenda of justice and peace and the well-being of creation?'

My media friends tell me that the news industry is a young person's game, with hundreds of media graduates pouring out of the new universities each year to become cheap labour for the multiplicity of news outlets.

The work culture of this burgeoning news industry is a get-the-story-or-you're-out kind of world. It's dominated by a dog-eat-dog survival of the fittest ethic, and is filled with people in their early twenties who will be lucky if they survive in the industry until they are thirty.

The news outlets increasingly serve a finance-driven agenda demanding more material at less cost. Many of these researchers, assistant producers and news gatherers have little guidance or mentorship or any space to think about what they are doing beyond the next story or the next deadline. It's little wonder that they end up cutting corners just to keep the show on the road.

As I made my way around the news studios of London during the unfolding Kember story, I took with me a pile of DVDs. Each DVD contained a twelve minute professionally made documentary about my visit to 'no man's land' between the armies of Eritrea and Ethiopia. It showed the Christians in the United Nations camp there, and told the story of the denial of religious freedom in Eritrea, of Christians' inhumane imprisonment in shipping containers in the desert by the Eritrean government and of their horrific torture in its prison camps.

Each of the dynamic young news researchers to whom I gave the DVDs assured me that they were interested in the story, and that they would put it forward as a potential item at their forward planning meetings. But despite my follow-up e-mails and calls, not one of the news channels took up the issue. I suppose that my film didn't have the kind of pull that they were looking for, or that there wasn't enough celebrity, entertainment value or pizzazz to make it work. Though the story carried enormously significant news about the trampling of human rights and the erosion of religious freedom, it did not seem to have the sensationalist or glamorous edge that contemporary journalists are trained to seek out.

It's important to go on seeking dialogue with the young

researchers and journalists of the media industry, even when the demands of their working environment mean that their priorities do not seem a close match to my own. They live in a tough world, and they need encouragement and the opportunity to talk reflectively about the pressurized environment in which they live. I have felt privileged in recent years to make their acquaintance, and to take the profile of an evangelical Christian out of the realm of stereotype and into the realm of human reality.

We must pray that God will place His representatives at the heart of the news industry in our nation. The church needs people who know how to play the media game, and who can bring a more balanced perspective. The news media are in urgent need of both salt and light.

If I am to 'do the right thing' in the media, I have to be aware of what is being packaged as 'news'. Many of the really important stories, the stories which are on God's heart, never make it into the news at all. I need also to become less judgmental about the people I see on the screen and the scandalous news I am told about them, recognising that many of them may have been misrepresented, their words and actions twisted or even falsified to create a more sensational impression.

I need to watch the news with less gullibility, to protest when I know they've got it wrong, and to keep speaking out about the stories which are never covered, and I must support those Christian pressure groups who care about the media, the truth and the oppressed.

Sex and celebrity

Christians believe that we lose our true perspective if we allow anything or anyone to take the number one spot in our life and relegate God to the sidelines. In a society besotted with celebrity, we can easily put other human beings on a pedestal, and even try to live our lives through their much publicised adventures. For many people, the cult of celebrity has become the focus of their existence. They are fascinated by the antics of the latest superstars but haven't the energy to develop their own identities and personalities. In an increasingly isolationist society, where people travel in solitude by car, shop on the internet, and often have never met their next-door-neighbours, film stars, soap characters and public figures sometimes replace the real relationships that have gone missing from our lives. This obsession with celebrity can easily become a form of idolatry, worshipping and focusing upon the stars the media have created, rather than the Creator himself.

Jesus taught that selflessness, service and sacrifice are the keys to true human fulfilment, whilst the media have conned us into thinking that status, superficiality and sex appeal are all that really matters.

In youth surveys it is apparent that the greatest ambition of the rising generation is to find 'star status' and to become celebrities in their own right. They want to be famous, to be known and to be respected. Maybe this indicates a deep need for reassurance of their real worth and uniqueness.

Some reality TV shows model the age-old concept that our identity lies in how other people perceive us, as if life were a matter of winning the approval of those who watch us live. But the Christian faith teaches that it is God who sees us, knows us and searches our hearts; God who travels alongside us and who will never let us go. What God thinks of us should be the real barometer for achievement and self-worth – and God loves us. A generation weaned on celebrity lifestyle, in which the few are chosen and the majority are left rejected and ashamed, will end up with a very warped understanding of who they are and what life is really about.

This kind of artificiality features strongly in *Big Brother*, where ordinary people are projected into stardom because of their seeming ability to gain a fan base from the millions watching. Yet despite the cult of celebrity and the ratings-driven focus on extreme behaviour, the audience watching at home will sometimes elect winners who model a gentler and more moderate way of living than most of the residents of the Big Brother House. The hearts of ordinary people still recognise and vote for goodness.

Craig Philips gave his money away to a girl who needed an operation, and the Christian called Cameron Stout refused to be drawn into the drunken games of the Big Brother House. He showed a high degree of integrity in his relationships and lifestyle, an attitude which was not for show, but which I have seen again and again as I have worked with him in the years since his appearance in the Big Brother House.

The quest for stardom has driven many thousands of young people to audition for reality shows like *Big Brother*, *How Do You Solve A Problem Like Maria?*, *The Apprentice*, or talent shows which promise recording contracts and celebrity status. This is cheap television to produce, and it offers great commercial opportunities for the companies making it. Talent shows do offer a moment to shine to many aspirational performers, and for the handful of winners may hold out a tremendous opportunity, but for the overwhelming majority of those who are successful in getting onto the shows, their fate will be merciless public humiliation for the amusement of a mass audience. The true human cost of this kind of entertainment can never be fully gauged, but it seems likely that some of the contestants may never fully recover from the ordeal.

Flicking channels earlier in the day I found subject matter covered for daytime viewing also disheartening at times. There is some excellent educational material for children, lots of fun and creativity, but there can be little doubt that small children are exposed to things which would have been unthinkable even twenty years ago. The whole concept of the watershed is now so weak as to be almost unnoticeable.

The availability of hardcore porn channels in millions of

homes has led to a steep rise in addiction to pornography. I'm convinced that in a civilised society there should be watersheds, film certificates and legal controls over what is screened. The link between what is shown on television and the growth in child abuse, rape and prostitution, already suggested by some academic studies, must be established beyond doubt.

A healthy view of sex has been denied to many because of their poor sense of self-worth, their lack of good parental role models and their dysfunctional family life. Negative childhood experiences have driven some to a search for intimacy and meaning in the dark, empty world of pornography.

Many Christians need to face up to their own addiction in this area, to realise that it is sinful and an offence which is against both God and themselves. They need to repent, ask the Holy Spirit for help and to block those channels which they know to be wrong.

Care, the Christian movement for a better society, has founded Covenant Eyes to help Christians to become stronger in their personal control over pornographic internet sites. The software package developed by the charity puts groups of Christians together and encourages relationships of accountability in the use of the internet.

A similar system for television digital systems is urgently needed. We should allow our Christian friends to check that the parental controls on our set-top boxes which lock out pornography are switched on, and that we use these controls which are so widely available yet so rarely used.

The enormity of this rising tide of hedonism and immorality is overwhelming. I find myself appalled at what is now shown as part of soaps, police series and serious drama. I hear myself muttering 'Disgusting... someone should be doing something about all this', but never getting round to doing anything about it myself.

Watchdogs and censorship

One night I turned on to BBC2 hoping to catch the end of *Newsnight,* when I came across a filmed report on some proposed legislation that interested me.

The report was on a programme which I later discovered was called *Desi DNA*: a multicultural view of the world with an earthy, alternative feel.

The reporter, walking through Soho, was describing the 'outdated legal system' which protects religious sensibilities. He went on to conclude that the laws of blasphemy are antiquated and irrelevant.

To reinforce his point, an audience had been invited to hear Hari Kunzra's controversial poem called 'The Love that dares to speak its name'. An actor began to recite the poem, and I couldn't believe that I was hearing such material on a mainstream terrestrial channel.

What followed was the most offensive, disgusting and sickening desecration of Jesus Christ and the cross, in which grotesque homosexual practices involving Jesus were graphically described.

I felt sick and hurt. I stumbled into my study, dialled the number for the BBC duty officer, and tried to explain to him why the programme was so deeply offensive to me.

About 30 minutes later I got to speak to a senior BBC manager, who noted my concerns in a very dispassionate tone. Several days later I received a three-paragraph letter stating that my complaint had been 'noted', but that after viewing the programme those in management had decided that it had been found my complaint was unsubstantiated.

It's clear to me that the BBC is not capable of policing its own programme makers, or of controlling its multifarious output. I'm convinced that there is a need for an independent body for arbitration to decide whether my licence fee can be spent on producing something which is blasphemous and deeply offensive.

But the BBC is not the only broadcaster which should be policed. The material available on the diverse array of satellite and digital channels available in the UK should also be under constant review. The excuse is made that the growth in the number of channels and the volume of output has now rendered censorship and watersheds beyond enforcement, and that the task is too great for any watchdog.

I find this impossible to accept in an age in which, we are told, millions of e-mails and thousands of phone calls are checked for terrorist links. The existence of so many channels suggests that there is a multi-million-pound market to fund them. A tax on the broadcast platforms, such as Sky and Freeview, should be able to finance the creation of watchdogs with teeth. Ofcom (the independent regulator and competition authority for the UK communications industries, with responsibilities across television, radio, telecommunications and wireless communications) might admirably fulfil such a function if better resourced.

Jerry Springer – The Opera, the show which put Jesus in a nappy and portrayed him and his family as utterly dysfunctional, was screened on BBC2. This controversial decision by the BBC raised important questions about censorship and proper control of the media.

It was screened without the BBC's Central Religious Advisory Committee (CRAC) having had the opportunity to comment, let alone the chance to see it. Had they done so, they might have been able to assess whether those defending the show were right in claiming that it was a poignant comment on reality television, that it condemned the exploitation of people in creating freak shows, and made a prophetic statement about the contemporary media.

Over recent years CRAC has seen shows only after they have been screened, so one has to ask whether the BBC really takes their existence seriously or views their insights as important.

The BBC received around 55,000 complaints about *Jerry*

Springer – The Opera prior to broadcast (including e-mails and telephone contacts) and approximately 8,000 complaints following transmission.

Over the weekend of its screening the BBC Press Office could not find one BBC executive, producer or manager to appear on my Premier Radio news show to defend their actions. It was a full two weeks before I was given access to Roland Keating, the Controller of BBC2. It seemed incredible to me that the BBC was so reticent to defend its actions before a largely Christian audience. As a public servant, the Corporation should have made a spokesperson available immediately.

Keating told me that his decision to screen the show was based solely on its 'significance' and 'artistic merit'. Only time will tell whether this awful production will be seen by future generations as significant or of lasting merit. The Christian religion is a particular media target for such programmes of satirical and cynical material. It is unlikely that a similar attack on Islam or the Sikh religion would have been countenanced.

Richard Tait, the Chair of the Governors' Programme Complaints Committee (GPCC), which met some weeks later to view the programme and to review the complaints, later reported that:

> The BBC is committed to freedom of expression and has a duty to innovate, to reflect new and challenging ideas and to make available to its audiences work of outstanding artistic significance. In all the circumstances, the outstanding artistic significance of the programme outweighed the offence which it caused to some viewers and so the broadcasting of the programme was justified.

To me, this was further evidence of the BBC's inability to police its own programme makers. One must question whether, in this process, they really acted in the spirit of their charter or whether their decisions were in keeping with the rules that they have set for themselves. When 55,000 complain but the programme goes ahead, does that not simply imply that the BBC is not really listening?

I would have had no objection to *Jerry Springer* being put on in the theatre. In that situation the audience makes a conscious decision to go and see the production. When it is broadcast at the licence fee payer's expense, however, and when it is broadcast by a Corporation with a charter which specifically mandates service of the wider community, a show of such content is inappropriate and unacceptable, even in a highly secularised country.

I would argue that the watchdog overseeing Independent Television has more bite, and that the Independent Television Commission might well have acted more swiftly, had such a show been broadcast on ITV.

I don't find it easy to 'do the right thing', when that means I am trying to make Roland Keating think through the implications of his decisions, phoning the duty officer or writing e-mails of complaint. It must be even harder when, like one BBC radio producer, you feel obliged to quit your job altogether in protest over *Jerry Springer – The Opera*; yet if we don't stand up for what we believe, put pressure on the TV executives who make the decisions, join groups who monitor media output, or give voice to our feelings in the press, the Christian conscience will soon be unheard and forgotten.

Unless the Christian community stands up for what it believes in and speaks out about what is and is not acceptable, it is unreasonable to expect the wider community and the makers of TV programmes to read our minds. Our critique must also accentuate the positive, applauding broadcasters when they make good, wholesome and helpful shows. Viewer response, both positive and negative, ultimately does feed into the complex decision-making process which creates the broadcast media.

The Temple of the Arts and Muses

I made my way into the plush West End hotel and was ushered into a bar which was hastily being transformed into a television studio. I had been invited to appear in a marathon TV special entitled *The 100 Greatest Christmas TV Moments*.

When the lights and cameras had been set, I was asked to view a programme on the huge screen before me. It was my favourite episode from *The Vicar of Dibley*, portraying an unexpected birth in a Nativity play in a stable. I roared with laughter.

The lights came on, 'Is this episode not blasphemy?' the young reporter snarled.

'No way,' I replied. 'Just very, very funny television.'

The lights went out again, and a scene from *Father Ted* appeared. He was hiding in the ladies' underwear department of a large Irish department store while trying to buy a Christmas present for his housekeeper. Some twenty other assorted priests were similarly hidden.

Again, I roared with laughter. 'What does this say about male Catholic sexuality?'

'Nothing,' I replied. 'But it says a lot about the awkwardness that many men feel in such a female domain.'

The interviewer was evidently disappointed that I wasn't going to fit the Christian stereotype that she had in mind!

It's sad that so many of us who claim to be Christian are categorised as narrow, boring and lacking any sense of humour. There is much to enjoy in contemporary television, and much to be applauded. Programmes like *Father Ted* and *The Vicar of Dibley* became hot favourites with the Christian viewing audience, who recognised and appreciated the hilarious portrayal of the oddities and idiosyncrasies peculiar to church life and tradition.

Documentaries such as *The Monastery*, *The Convent*, *God bless Ibiza* and *The Romance Academy* have shown Christian television at its very best. They have somehow captured

Christian witness as having great integrity and power; and anyone watching the influence of the Christians in these series will have been aware of moments in which the sense of God's presence was most powerfully felt, both on-screen and in our living rooms at home. These programmes also helpfully exposed the real interface between religious tradition and the seekers and pilgrims abounding in the wider community. They showed that the human search for meaning continues vitally both inside and outside the church, and that modern, sophisticated people still thirst for the wellspring of truth they can feel and trust.

For both regular church-goers and many who never attend church worship, *Songs of Praise* has been a point of contact with the believing community, and a source of hope and inspiration. For thousands who are kept at home by shyness, disability, family commitment or frailty of age, it is the primary, or only, opportunity to participate in worship. I'm grateful to the leaders such as Gerald Coates, however, who have fought long and hard for this last bastion of Christian prime time witness to be saved.

Over the years I have pitched programme ideas to television executives and producers in many different contexts. Occasionally, I've felt the breath of the Spirit, and doors have opened suddenly and miraculously – like the day I persuaded ITV to take a 40 man TV crew to Enniskillen to film a Remembrance Day Service, and then persuaded Lady Diana to come too! That show was not only transmitted live throughout the UK by ITV but around the world by CNN!

But there have been many, many other days when I have left the offices of the BBC and independent producers feeling that the door was firmly shut for Christian programming in the mainstream media. My commitment to Christian programming through many years on Premier Radio and my five series on the God Channel were born out of a deep frustration in failing to get the message onto the mainstream channels.

I hope and pray that a new generation of visionary young

Christians will seize the new opportunities emerging through the multiplicity of new channels and platforms. But there is also much to be concerned about. If we are to do the right thing we need to campaign on behalf of those whose sensitivity to explicit violence and sex is gradually being eroded.

I'm convinced that the never ending stream of violent and sexual images is fuelling crime, promoting dysfunctional relationships and commercially exploiting teen culture.

The Christian community must make a stand for purity and goodness in the interests of our children and grandchildren. If we don't do so we can only anticipate an even worse form of television taking standards to unimaginable levels of depravity.

> For we wrestle not against flesh and blood, but against principalities, against powers, against the rulers of the darkness of this world, against spiritual wickedness in high places (Ephesians 6:12).

The worldview of many Christians today has been shaped by the media rather than by the Word of God. We have become dedicated followers of culture, rather than allowing our thoughts and lifestyle to be shaped by Jesus Christ.

The time has come to remember Paul's call in the letter to the Romans (12:2, ESV): 'Do not conform any longer to the pattern of this world, but be transformed by the renewing of your mind. Then you will be able to test and approve what God's will is – his good, pleasing and perfect will.'

When the BBC was first founded by Lord Reith, he had some words from the Bible inscribed in marble in the entrance hall of Broadcasting House in 1931 so that everyone could see it. They remain there to this day. He wrote:

> This Temple of the Arts and Muses is dedicated to Almighty God by the first Governors of Broadcasting ... It is their prayer

that good seed sown may bring forth a good harvest, that all things hostile to peace and purity may be banished from this house and that the people, inclining their ear to whatsoever things are beautiful, and honest and of good report, may tread a path of wisdom and uprightness.

If we can no longer trust those in editorial control to ensure that the vision which Lord Reith had is remembered and upheld, it's all the more crucial that we take personal editorial control over our eyes, ears and minds.

Paul reminds us that 'everything is lawful but not everything is desirable'. We need to be tuned in to the Holy Spirit as clearly as to the media. We must ask Him to remind us when the things we see or hear are not desirable, or are destructive.

It is vital that we exercise responsibility over what we watch and hear and encourage our children and grandchildren to do the same. Indiscriminate television viewing may be doing us serious damage; and it's up to us to learn how the 'off' button works.

Discussion Questions

1 This is the contemporary news environment. It is being created as we watch. No time to think, or plan, or weigh up the alternatives. Only the constant drive to get the latest breaking story on the screen before the competition. What effect does this kind of pressure have on the news agenda?

2 In a contest between celebrity and poverty, celebrity wins hands down every time. In what ways do we or might we draw the reality and agenda of the life of poor and struggling people to the attention of the media audience?

3 If conflict draws an audience, disagreement is interesting and strongly held views from different perspectives make good entertainment, what does this do to news programmes? Some feel that modern media interview techniques are too aggressive and antagonistic – what are your feelings about this?

4 Documentaries such as *The Monastery, The Convent, God Bless Ibiza* and *The Romance Academy* have given positive coverage of the Christian faith, at the same time as being television at its very best. Did you see any of them? What impact did they make on you? What examples of good programmes do you treasure?

5 What do you think about the entertainment value of reality shows like *Big Brother, How do you Solve a Problem like Maria?, The Apprentice*, and talent shows which promise recording contracts and celebrity status? How might they change the lives of the participants?

6 We live in a society that values freedom of expression; and as it strives to portray intense moments of reality, art can often present images that are disturbing or extreme. In the context of television and radio, what do you think should determine the boundaries to this freedom? In what ways might exposure to scenes of explicit sex and violence affect patterns of life in the family and in wider society?

7 What kind of regulation would you like to see imposed upon the makers of television programmes? How might this be

conceived and enforced – or are you satisfied with the system already in place?

8 'This Temple of the Arts and Muses is dedicated to Almighty God by the first Governors of Broadcasting ... It is their prayer that good seed sown may bring forth a good harvest, that all things hostile to peace and purity may be banished from this house and that the people, inclining their ear to whatsoever things are beautiful, and honest and of good report, may tread a path of wisdom and uprightness.' This was Lord Reith's vision for the broadcast media – what's yours?

9 Paul reminds us that 'everything is lawful but not everything is desirable.' In your experience, what is good to watch – and what is harmful?

Chapter Six

Doing the Right Thing in a Politically Correct Age

An age of diminishing freedom

Thirty years ago, when I was a student at theological college, the Principal called me into his office and asked me to look after a young Macedonian church minister called Kitan who had come to the UK to study. He spoke little English, and was struggling to cope with the pressures of University life.

Kitan became a close friend, and over the course of the year I learnt about the challenges of his life back home. He had been frequently harassed by the police, forbidden to hold evangelistic meetings, and sometimes interrogated and imprisoned for his illegal church-planting activities in a sensitive communist state. He would preach for an hour at funerals because this was one of the few occasions when he could speak freely and without threat of imprisonment!

At the end of our year together a group of us took Kitan home to Macedonia in our twelve-year-old minibus. It was a very long journey and a great adventure, during which we literally had to push it up the Alps. Later, at a secret smuggling depot in Trieste, we filled it with illegal Macedonian Bibles for the churches of that troubled land.

One of the most frightening experiences of my life was approaching the border and waiting for the guards to search us for illegal contraband! Although they took to pieces the car in the queue before us, searching it for almost an hour, they simply waved us through without so much as a glance at our illegal stock of Bibles stacked high on the seats of the minibus! Our prayer to 'make seeing eyes blind' was clearly answered that day.

I will never forget distributing those Macedonian Bibles in the middle of a forest very early one morning. Christians who were desperate for the word of God gradually appeared through the mist, desperate for their own copy. I have never forgotten those people, nor the persecution which they endured for their love of the Gospel. One senior minister whom we met there had been in and out of prison for his faith many times. He gripped my hand and said:

> In the west the trees are lush and green. They stand tall and proud and close together. Here the trees stand alone, gnarled and weather beaten, made strong by wind and weather. But when the strong winds come the lush trees all collapse, while the gnarled old trees stand firm. Beware, for the Christians in the west have not endured as we have. And now, sadly, they are not as strong.

The suffering of Christians like them has often been the mainspring for the renewal of the church. When I first became a Christian I did not understand that such suffering was integral to our calling. Suffering is part of what it means to follow Christ, and we suffer for Him in celebration of the way that He suffered for us.

Over the years which have elapsed since my student days, Kitan has witnessed the collapse of communism, the legalisation of evangelism and the meteoric rise to Prime Minister of one of his church congregation! So much changed, so quickly!

I am currently the President of Release International, an organisation which cares for the persecuted church around the world, and has brought me into renewed contact with Christians in many different parts of the world who are enduring persecution for their faith.

This work has lead me to think more about the kind of world in which I live and minister here in the UK; and to begin to consider how contemporary societal trends are affecting Christian witness in Great Britain. Gradually I have come to the conclusion that the erosion of Christian freedom in the UK is accelerating so quickly that, unless British Christians orchestrate an organised and sustained response, we may in our turn come to face persecution.

I remember watching one summer's evening as Kitan preached in the open air in this country, tears streaming down his face as he recognised that he was enjoying a kind of freedom never known at that time in Macedonia. Kitan recognised how precious was the privilege of such freedom; it is incumbent upon us to work for and defend continued freedom. We must act decisively against the trend towards both silencing and restricting religious expression and enhancing and encouraging the freedom of secular denigration of religious belief.

An age of secularisation

Thirty years ago when I first worked in hospital chaplaincy I was welcomed as a member of the medical team. I was given access to confidential information, and notified of every new admission. In many hospitals, like the one where I was an inpatient recently, this is now a thing of the past. Information legislation now prevents such free access to patient lists; chaplains today rely upon church members to pass on details of new Christian inpatients, and upon regular ward rounds, where they may encounter those who would appreciate a visit.

Thirty years ago I regularly preached in the open air, and the relevant permit was usually granted as a formality. In a recent request for police help I was threatened with arrest should I continue with a planned march of witness because it might constitute a breach of the peace. We went ahead anyway, and the event was a great occasion which, thank God, passed without incident.

I have led evangelistic missions in scores of towns and cities throughout the United Kingdom. Some of these have been in areas with large Asian populations, such as Bradford, Southall and the Lancashire mill towns. In these missions we have often partnered with Asian congregations and seen how the joint witness of Christians from British and Asian backgrounds can be a powerful witness to good race relations. Out of hundreds of personal contacts between our teams and local people I never received a single complaint.

Then a couple of years ago a mainstream church denomination refused to welcome our mission teams to Birmingham because this activity was considered inappropriate for such a multicultural context. One church leader informed me that the arrival of such teams would be 'derogatory to good race relations,' even though we had promised that all the teams would receive racism awareness training and be multicultural in their mix.

Does this mean that the UK is now sub-divided into areas suitable for Christian mission and others which are too sensitive for such an activity? And if so, what does this say about the future of evangelism in the UK and the freedom of religious expression which I thought was an integral part of a pluralist culture?

An age of multi-faith education

At one time, I would not have thought twice about the content of my talk in a school assembly. I would have considered it quite acceptable that I could refer to Jesus as Christ, divide time into the eras AD and BC, speak of miracles and of salvation, and express my heartfelt personal belief that Christ is the only way to God.

In a multicultural and multi-faith context it would be

considered inappropriate to do the same today. It would appear that such freedoms are now being seriously questioned – even in church schools.

Recently the Church of England faced criticism about the use of meditation in school assemblies in an article in the *New Statesman*. Nick Cohen, the writer, said that schools in one diocese were being encouraged to use techniques similar to hypnosis to focus children's minds in lessons.

On the Radio 4 *Today* programme the Church of England dismissed as 'nonsense' reports that some of its schools were brainwashing children during religious education lessons. The Right Revd Kenneth Stevenson, Bishop of Portsmouth, told the BBC that the article had 'twisted' and 'distorted' teaching guidance on the use of meditation in class notes issued to Church of England schools by the Diocese of Canterbury.

Bishop Stevenson, the chairman of the Church of England Board of Education, rejected suggestions that pupils were put in 'trance-like' states during classroom meditation sessions. He told the programme: 'They [pupils] do what many adults do – sit quietly and think.' He added: 'It's quite a legitimate exercise for schools to do on a voluntary basis.'

A Church of England spokesman said the practice of meditation had been used in the church and in other religions and belief systems for centuries. 'It's a way of thinking about things. As for brainwashing, it's not about closing people's minds. This is about opening people's minds to think about things and look at lots of subjects, not simply about God. Meditation is making space to focus on God's creation. It's making you concentrate on what is going on.'

I find it incredible that the practice of Christian meditation is being condemned in the context of a church school curriculum. Research indicates that church schools often produce a higher standard of education than many of their secular counterparts. In recent years, however, there has been an increasing suspicion about their ethos and growth.

The Archbishop of Canterbury has defended Muslim and other faith schools and insisted they were 'nothing to apologise for'. Dr Rowan Williams said the 'good following wind' for faith schools had, regrettably, changed after 9/11.

In a major speech on education Dr Williams said Muslims and members of other faiths should be able to continue to set up their own schools, which are eligible for state funding and support. The alternative was that people of different religions would become 'more isolated and ghettoised'.

Dr Williams described the sharply contrasting approaches to education. 'There is a real tension in educational thinking between those whose concern is primarily, almost exclusively, with imparting skills to individuals and those who understand education as something that forms the habits of living in a group, identifying common aspirations and making possible co-operation and conversation.' He stressed that the ethos of church schools was of the latter type.

We can only hope and pray that the 'good following wind' to the growth and development of Christian and church-based schools will return. Such schools have much to add to the richness and quality of our education system.

Nor does the path of the faithful run smooth in higher education. Take, for instance, the work of a group which called itself Faiths Together on Campus, a partnership that included the Catholic Student Council, the Federation of Student Islamic Societies, the National Union of Students, the Union of Jewish Students and the Student Christian Movement, with a stated objective of bringing together Catholic, Islamic, Christian, Jewish, Hindu and Sikh societies at universities in an attempt to create religious tolerance and respect. Yet it seemed that the tolerance and respect did not extend to the evangelical wing of the Christian faith.

Faiths Together on Campus gathered round an agenda overtly antagonistic to Christian Unions in universities across the UK. The draft paper from this group bracketed

Christian Unions and the Christian Medical Fellowship together with cults which use brainwashing techniques, arguing that because these evangelical Christian organisations insisted that student leaders of Christian Unions assented to a doctrinal statement, they were flouting the 1998 Human Rights Act.

The paper argued that requirement for a doctrinal statement enabled extreme factions to keep a stranglehold over certain student religious societies, and that it stifled variation of opinion. This group intended to 'monitor religious toleration on campuses' and produced a Code of Practice insisting that no religious organisation should discriminate in their rules for either membership or leadership on grounds of religious belief!

Happily, public opinion and extensive publicity in the Christian media led to the demise of this aggressive initiative. It is surprising that the leaders and convenors of Faiths Together on Campus, such passionate advocates for human rights and religious freedoms, were unaware that Article 9 of the European Convention on Human Rights gives all religions the inherent legal right to propagate their faith, and that Section 43 of the Education Act of 1986 gives religious groups protection to evangelise because it is a form of freedom of speech. Basic human rights law recognises the principle of 'freedom of association'. It teaches that one of those rights is to exclude people from our organisations if they do not subscribe to our fundamental principles.

Even the Magna Carta of 1215 reads: 'We have confirmed for us and our heirs in perpetuity that the English Church shall be free and shall have its right undiminished and its liberty unimpaired.'

The heart of the problem in this confrontation was the familiar human tendency to a particular blind spot. Faiths Together On Campus believes passionately in religious freedom and tolerance – for everybody who agrees with them;

and sometimes that kind of blind spot has afflicted evangelical Christians as well.

An age of Gay Pride

Homophobia leads to discriminatory and sometimes violent behaviour. It is an irrational prejudice against someone because of their homosexual orientation or practice. There can be no excuse for Christians to be homophobic or to treat homosexuals in a critical, cynical or violent way. The Bible teaches that we should love our neighbours as ourselves – regardless of their sexual orientation.

Yet Christians are also called to be true to the teachings of the Bible and to their faith. As a result, most (if not all) Christians accept the traditional understanding of the church that the only rightful sexual relationship intended by God is between a man and a woman in a monogamous marriage. If people hold to this view it may well imply that they are Bible believing Christians; but it doesn't necessarily follow that they are homophobic. The fundamental human freedom to hold this view as part of our religious belief system is an important aspect of religious freedom.

Despite this, liberal Christians and many contributing to the debate from outside the church insist that Christians who teach that homosexuality is not acceptable are inevitably homophobic. The difference of opinion centres around the question of whether ethics and morality can ever be purely personal. It is unlikely that anybody would object to a Christian of homosexual orientation choosing to be celibate in order to uphold the traditional teaching of the church and the Bible. The problem occurs when Christians are perceived as criticising the life choices of other people, and is exacerbated when those who take this traditional, biblical view stand firm on the point that it must remain normative for the whole Christian communion – even for those who disagree. This difference of approach is sharply focused in conflicts on many university campuses around the UK, where antagonism has arisen between Student Unions and Christian Unions on this issue.

In Warwick the Christian Union was banned from the campus because its members were deemed to have failed to comply with the university's anti-discrimination legislation. A hoax e-mail was sent to the CU President asking for pastoral advice on homosexuality, and the President framed a polite and compassionate reply, quoting the CU's biblical stand, but also making it clear that other Christians had different views. His reply was used by members of the Warwick Student Union to prove that the CU did not comply with the University's equal opportunities policies and were therefore unfit to use the facilities of the Student Union. They have had to meet off campus ever since.

In Birmingham the Student Union took exception to the moral teaching of the Christian Union, sequestering its funds, and banning its members from using Union facilities already booked for a major mission on the campus. Only strong action from the Lawyers' Christian Fellowship, a judicial review and the swift intervention of the university authorities secured the release of their funds. Thankfully, the mission was able to proceed in a marquee on ground not owned by the Student Union, and it even appears to have benefited from all the publicity!

Similar problems have been reported in Edinburgh, where a Christian 'Sex and Morality Course' supporting traditional Christian sexual morality being taught by members of the Christian Union was deemed inappropriate to be based at the university. The Christian Union were asked to withdraw from the campus.

In Bath, the Christian Union's teaching on sexuality led to questions about its constitution being raised in the Student's Union. As the Christian Union permits only Christians to hold internal leadership roles, the Student's Union judged that the organisation was discriminating against the rights of others by excluding them from the Christian Union committee. (In the interests of equality perhaps the Conservative Club should be led by members of the Socialist Party!)

Despite this campaign to remove Christian Unions from the universities, their long established witness continues. In fact, some report that these difficulties have actually led to stronger Christian Unions and a more effective level of witness. Christian students are beginning to stand up for their religious freedom, even taking legal advice where it has been deemed appropriate.

I support them wholeheartedly. This conflict is nothing to do with whether homosexuality is right or wrong. It has everything to do with whether Christians can continue to teach the traditional faith or not. These students are at the sharp end of Christian witness, and if they don't stand up for their religious freedom it will be snatched away for ever.

But problems over traditional Christian views on homosexuality have not been limited to universities. Rocco Buttiglione, a prominent and conservative Roman Catholic, caused a constitutional crisis when he was almost appointed as the European Commissioner for Justice.

In one of the committee hearings regarding his appointment he said that he 'regarded homosexuality as a sin'. This former philosophy professor and friend of the Pope affirmed: 'I have the right to think that homosexuality is a sin. But this has no effect on politics because in politics the principle of non-discrimination prevails.'

Buttiglione, whose proposed appointment threatened the appointment of the entire commission, claimed that he had been the victim of 'an anti-Catholic inquisition'. Does this mean that a conservative Roman Catholic is no longer welcome in the corridors of European power? Could he not practise his faith and still uphold principles of justice and equality?

Roman Catholics have also been in the spotlight over the closure of all their adoption agencies in the UK. The Sexual

Orientation Regulations, passed by the UK government in March 2007, started out with good intentions. They were designed to stamp out discrimination against practising gay and lesbian citizens in the provision of goods and services. I wholeheartedly support the good intent of this legislation, because discrimination against anyone on grounds of age, race, religion, sex or sexual orientation is completely unacceptable in a sophisticated and developed society.

Unfortunately, despite a massive campaign by thousands of committed Christians, the legislation does not take into account the religious understanding and beliefs of many committed believers. Whilst it is true that 'Regulation 14' does offer a substantial degree of protection to churches and to other religious organisations that are not 'solely or mainly commercial', there are still many ways in which Christians could fall foul of this new law. It's important to realise that this is a civil law, but when someone claims damages against a person or organisation which has 'discriminated' against a practising homosexual the sums levied as damages could be substantial.

So, for example, where previously the Roman Catholic adoption agencies have carried out a superb ministry in placing often difficult candidates for adoption with married couples throughout the UK, they must now comply with the Sexual Orientation Regulations. In other words, they must be willing to place a child in the home of two men or women who are practising homosexuals. Failure to do so would leave them open to lawsuits for discrimination, and ultimately to very expensive court settlements. As a result Cardinal Cormac Murphy-O'Connor has announced that all of the Catholic adoption agencies will have to close. A great piece of Christian service and ministry has been terminated, simply because no religious conscience clause was permitted in this legislation.

Furthermore, any church which receives State or Council funding for pieces of social action or service must now comply with these regulations. So if a church received a grant to run a shelter for the homeless, but did not comply with the regulations, it would be open to a civil action in the courts and the fairly immediate withdrawal of all funding.

The regulations assume that homosexual civil partnerships are fully equivalent to heterosexual marriages and that any provision of goods and services to married couples must also be provided equally to homosexual civil partners.

If, for example, Christians who run bed and breakfast businesses allow married heterosexual couples to book double rooms they will be acting illegally if they refuse to allow homosexual couples in civil partnerships to do the same.[1]

The remit of these regulations also extends to schools, making it illegal for the Local Education Authority or the Governors of a school to subject a pupil to 'any other detriment' by discriminating on the grounds of their sexual orientation. Undoubtedly there will be an enormous amount of debate in the courts in the years to come as the interpretation of the word 'detriment' is clarified.

What seems clear is that the school curriculum does come under these regulations, and that all schools (including church schools and Christian schools) will have to comply with them. Some lawyers believe that it will be unlawful to teach that practising homosexuality is wrong, and that marriage can't be promoted unless civil partnerships are given equal prominence and recognition.

These regulations pose many difficult questions for church leaders. On the one hand we need to affirm the rights

---

1 This issue is more complex than it first appears. Many Christians may see being gay as a sin, but surely the one thing they can be certain of is that all their customers will be sinners. Have they checked the marriage licences of their heterosexual customers? Will they be similarly excluding customers who are cruel or untruthful? Will they want to exclude Muslim customers and Jehovah's Witness customers because they too take a different view of the Bible? This issue appears straightforward, but it is by no means so in reality.

of all citizens to be treated equally, and to recognise that some homosexuals are themselves Christian. On the other hand we need to affirm the rights of Christians to hold to traditional biblical views on homosexuality.

An age of multicultural communities

Many Christians in the UK were greatly relieved when the religious hatred legislation put before Parliament in February 2006 failed to become law by one vote. This legislation, designed to promote harmony between the faiths, would have had exactly the reverse effect to that which was intended. Many are dismayed that the government has promised to re-introduce this legislation at the earliest opportunity.

Concerns about this legislation are best illustrated through the effect of similar (but not identical) legislation which is already law in Australia. The experience of Pastor Nalliah and Pastor Scot, two Christian leaders in Melbourne, has been like an unfolding nightmare.

They hosted a teaching seminar for 250 Christians, on the theme of Islam, as part of the ministry of Melbourne Pentecostal Church called Catch the Fire Ministries. The content of this conference was reported to the Equal Opportunities Commission. The legal case emanating from this complaint led to a test case involving the Islamic Council of Victoria v Catch The Fire Ministries, costing more than $1 million in legal fees and doing nothing to encourage trust or understanding between the different religious groups involved.

Leading politician Peter Costello, tipped to be a future Australian prime minister, referred to the case in a speech in May 2004 in which he said:

I do not think that we should resolve differences about religious views in our community with lawsuits between the different religions. Nor do I think that the object of religious harmony will be promoted by organising witnesses to go along to the meetings of other religions to collect evidence for the purpose of later litigation.

The proceedings which have been taken [under this new law], the time, the cost, the extent of the proceedings, and the remedies that are available – all illustrate, in my view, that this is a bad law.

The effect on the Christian ministers, who claim that the information shared at the seminar was purely factual, cannot be easily estimated. 'This has caused us a tremendous amount of time and stress,' said Pastor Danny Nalliah, the head of Catch The Fire Ministries, in a press statement.

Peter Costello concluded: 'Tolerance under the law is a great part of this tradition. Tolerance does not mean that all views are the same. It does not mean that differing views are equally right. What it means is that where there are differences, no matter how strongly held, different people will respect the right of others to hold them.'

I believe the sanity and good sense of these remarks are equally applicable to life in Great Britain.

If the experience of our Christian friends in Australia is to be replicated here, the reintroduction of religious hatred legislation in the UK will lead to a rapid deterioration of what has been a creative and healthy culture of inter-faith dialogue. The introduction of such legislation in the UK will do nothing to improve race relations.

It's important that the different faiths work together in maintaining high standards of religious tolerance and freedom. Harmony between different racial, religious and cultural groups is much more likely to result from good working relationships and the identification of shared values than from legislation which can do nothing but increase their suspicions of one another!

An age of intolerance

When Alexis de Tocqueville wrote *Democracy in America* (1835–9) he concluded that there can be a 'tyranny of the majority'. De Tocqueville observed that 'democratic majorities' can significantly oppress minorities, indulging in tyrannical activities of suppression and expropriation. Moreover, this could all, in a democracy, be apparently 'legal' since a thoroughgoing democratic state would subordinate all avenues of redress and protection to the majority.

Christian lawyer Michael Ovey, writing about the 'tyranny of majorities', concluded that 'Christians cannot give unqualified commitments to obey majorities.' If they did, that amounts to saying the majority has no overlord and either derives its power legitimacy from something other than God or simply from itself. Such absolute commitments amount to complicity in the tyranny – to use the word in an extended sense – of majoritarian supremacy.

Jesus Christ was a radical revolutionary and his initial followers were a tiny minority. As we in the UK rediscover what it means to be a tiny minority, we must not make the mistake of thinking that the majority is always right. On the contrary, we need to rediscover what it means to be salt and light, and how we can affect the whole even when we are vastly outnumbered! As we become an identified minority within the British population we must leave behind the old assumptions about our importance, influence and prestige and move towards a new role and a new opportunity.

We must become more outspoken, challenging those ideas and popular trends which are unbiblical and dangerous. This may lead us into direct confrontation with political institutions, societal structures and legal authorities; and some of us will find this a personally costly activity.

Just because we are a minority does not mean that we are excluded from the rights and privileges of any minority group within a pluralist society. In fact, we should make confident claim on those rights which are fairly ours. We have the right of freedom of speech and we have a right to believe, to worship, to serve and to proselytise.

Yet in the babble of voices claiming justice for their particular cause or faith community the Christian church has often been silent and invisible. We have an historic right of freedom of speech which means that we are free to proclaim the uniqueness and divinity of Jesus Christ in the pulpit, in the street and through printed and electronic media. While we must also affirm the importance of other minority groups to their equivalent rights, we have a responsibility to see that the creeds of the church are appropriately represented in striking the balance that will preserve social harmony, freedom and peace.

For many of us the balance between rights and freedoms is in jeopardy. Whilst I affirm your right to engage in homosexual practice, you must defend my freedom to believe that the Bible teaches something different. Whilst I affirm your right to build a mosque in my neighbourhood, you must defend my freedom to practise my evangelism. Whilst I affirm your right to publish literature derogatory to Christianity, you must allow me the freedom to say that there is no salvation outside of Jesus Christ. Whilst I affirm your right to claim state funding for a social work project driven by an atheistic worldview, I expect the freedom to apply for similar funding for Christian projects. Whilst I affirm your right to run a Hindu school which teaches your religion, I defend the freedom to extend the influence of church schools wherever people want them.

There is an argument to be won and some basic principles of contemporary citizenship in a pluralist society to be claimed. This is not something just for the politicians and lawyers. It's a task which must engage all of us, in every sphere of contemporary life. It's about teachers having the right to teach the Christian story, and hospital chaplains claiming the right to know the names of churchgoing patients, and Christian Unions being allowed to remain part of the university community. It's about broadcasters being able to reflect true Christian values, evangelists going unhindered about their ministry, and managers having the freedom to decline the opportunity to attend New Age training seminars. It's about employers having the freedom to take on the person best suited for the task and preachers proclaiming the undiluted message without fear of spies with notebooks in the congregation.

These freedoms are being eroded when we don't use them. They disappear when we give up before defending our freedoms. It's time we learnt how to lobby Parliament when Bills such as the 'religious hatred' legislation appear. We need to raise up a legal fundwhich will be ready to support lawyers to fight crucial test cases on behalf of the Christian community.

We need to become a little more outspoken, a little less cowardly, and a lot more confident! There is something we can all do if we just think about it. And if we are freedom-fighters empowered by God, we can make a difference – not only for our own generation, but for all the generations yet to come! Going against the stream, standing out from the crowd and facing opposition and persecution go with the territory for those who would follow Jesus.

One day Zebedee's wife came to ask Jesus if James and John could be promoted, one to sit on His right, and the other on His left. She wanted them to occupy privileged positions of power in the coming kingdom.

Her question revealed how little she understood about His teaching and how limited was her knowledge about the manner of His coming. Jesus turned to James and John, and asked them: 'Can you drink the cup of suffering that I am about to drink?' Jesus needed to make clear that an implicit part of their call was their willingness to suffer for their faith.

I have to admit that when I first became a Christian no-one made it clear to me that this kind of suffering was such an integral part of the discipleship package. Don't get me wrong, from the outset I heard great stories of the men and women of faith who suffered and even died for Jesus – but I can't recall anyone telling me that I should realistically expect to suffer for Christ myself.

It seemed to be news for James and John, too. Apparently they took the challenge, because in Acts 12:2 we read that Herod 'had James, the brother of John, put to death with the sword.' Historians believe that James was the first of the twelve to suffer martyrdom when he was killed in Jerusalem under the persecution instigated by Herod Agrippa.

The small Ethiopian Airways turbo-prop circled the grass airstrip. Minutes before, a lone herdsman had been driving his buffalo across the runway.

We circled again and made our final approach. The plane bounced and thumped its way across the field. Glad to be on 'terra firma' I walked down the plane's steps into the stifling heat. Before me with their large blue flags was a line of United Nations vehicles racing towards the airstrip. A UN helicopter was standing by. A line of top military officials emerged from the vehicles, saluted each other and climbed aboard the helicopter.

I had arrived in a very sensitive area. Thousands of Ethiopian troops were 'dug in' near the border with Eritrea, and just a few kilometres away the Eritreans were also preparing for war, while the United Nations organisation was struggling to maintain the fragile peace between the two countries. On the plane I had read in the newspaper that the previous day the Eritreans had threatened to shoot down UN helicopters approaching their border.

The purpose of my trip was to visit a refugee camp run by the United Nations and the Ethiopian authorities. It's right near the border, nestling in a tree lined valley between the two enormous armies. The six hour journey there in a clapped out minibus was one of the most uncomfortable of my life. We pitched and tossed our way over pot-holes, past dreadful traffic accidents and between miles of marching soldiers in full combat kit. After protracted negotiations with local officials the washing-line barrier was dropped, and we began the final 13 kilometre off-road safari to the refugee camp. Some 8,000 people live there on a subsistence diet provided by the UN, and the camp grows in size every day.

There, in the camp, it was my privilege to preach at the Tuesday night prayer service. The tin-roofed chapel was packed to the doors with a congregation of well over 200. The people worshipped and danced with great freedom and joy. It was the best praise time I'd been to in months. It was a young congregation, with most of the worshippers in the 18–30 age group. Many of the songs were the same as those you'll be singing in church on Sunday, though in their local language.

The service ended, and we made our way by torchlight between the scores of mud huts hastily built by the refugees themselves. The senior pastor welcomed me to his hut, and lit the oil lamp. He then proceeded to take off my shoes and socks and to wash my feet. I was choked with emotion.

During my time in the camp I interviewed a sample of fifteen Christians. Each interview lasted around 45 minutes, and I took detailed statements including names, places and dates. Some of the interviewees spoke excellent English, and others communicated through the interpreter who had travelled with me. I felt like some kind of detective trying to piece together an almost unbelievable story. All of the statements tallied. I am convinced that what they told me was true.

The Eritrean government states in its constitution that it embraces the principle of religious freedom. That freedom, however, seems to extend only to Christians who are Orthodox or Lutheran. The evangelical, charismatic and cell churches are all labelled 'pentie' – and the treatment of them has been appalling.

First the government insisted that all churches believed to be 'pentie' close down temporarily whilst they applied for state licences. They were asked to fill out forms, declare their aims, and to name their leadership. No licences were ever issued, but the government and the secret police gained much valuable information in the process. The evangelical churches were left with no alternative but to go under-ground. According to Amnesty International, over 200 church leaders were imprisoned during October 2005, though some have now been released. Many of those work-ing with Tearfund in projects to feed hungry children were also imprisoned for some time.

In Eritrea most men are conscripted into the army until age 40, and women until their first child is born. Many of the brightest young people go to a university which is run like a military academy. The government became concerned at the massive spread of evangelical Christianity in the armed forces, and especially at the academy.

Papers were produced whereby anyone suspected of hav-ing 'pentie' sympathies was asked to sign a declaration. It read 'I will not pray to Jesus, I will not read the Bible, I will not attend worship services other than Orthodox or Lutheran.' Those who refused to sign were taken to military prisons.

They were never tried in open court, never given the opportunity to make a defence or to claim their constitu-tional rights of religious freedom. They were, in a sense, court-martialled for their faith. Those who continued to practise their faith in military prisons were sent to special detention centres. These consisted of disused shipping containers in the desert, or labour camps where they had to dig wells in intense desert heat. I heard terrible stories of tor-ture, beating, solitary confinement and humiliation from both men and women. And all because they loved Jesus.

Some of those in the refugee camp had escaped from prison and simply run for their lives. Some had seen the police coming to arrest them and had fled with only what they were wearing. And some had signed the form after two or three years in prison. It was heart-rending to hear them say 'I failed Jesus, I let him down and I signed the form.' I hugged them. I'm sure that they had sacrificed more for the faith than I have ever done. I was humbled by their grace, their joy and their humility. They literally had nothing, and yet seemed to have everything.

Ultimately, doing the right thing can be very costly. And we need to take our lead from those Christians throughout history, and from around the world of whom Jesus said: 'Blessed are the persecuted.'

Discussion Questions

1 What have you noticed or experienced concerning religious freedom in your country? What changes in attitudes have you noticed in this area of life?

2 What kinds of Christian mission would you support, and what kinds would you consider inappropriate? Would you get involved in Christian mission in an Islamic neighbourhood? If so, what form would you like to see the mission take?

3 Archbishop Rowan Williams said Muslims and members of other faiths should be able to continue to set up their own schools, which are eligible for state funding and support. What are your thoughts about faith schools?

4 Some lawyers believe that it will be unlawful for schools to teach as part of any school syllabus that it is wrong to practise homosexuality, and that marriage cannot be promoted unless civil partnerships are given equal prominence and recognition. What do you feel about this? The Magna Carta of 1215 reads: 'We have confirmed for us and our heirs in perpetuity that the English Church shall be free and shall have its right undiminished and its liberty unimpaired...' Of what relevance are these words in modern, multi-faith society? Are there any ways in which you feel it should be updated for the contemporary scene?

5 If Christians teach that homosexual partnerships are unacceptable, is this homophobic? What is homophobia, and what is the difference between homophobia and standing up for biblical morality?

6 What place do the courts of law have in defending the right of Christians to express their religious belief? The teaching of the Bible is that differences between Christians should be settled without recourse to law (1 Corinthians 6:1–8) – but what about occasions when it is Christian traditional belief itself which comes under attack?

7 Cardinal Cormac Murphy-O'Connor has announced that all of the Catholic adoption agencies will have to close, terminating

a socially important ministry and service because the new Sexual Orientation Regulations and the moral standards of the Catholic Church cannot find an acceptable working compromise. What are your views on this dilemma?

8 The Australian politician, Peter Costello, said: 'Tolerance under the law is a great part of this tradition. Tolerance does not mean that all views are the same. It does not mean that differing views are equally right. What it means is that where there are differences, no matter how strongly held, different people will respect the right of others to hold them.' If you were asked to write a national constitution, what clauses might you include about tolerance in society? Creating social harmony involves getting the balance right between rights and freedoms, between what we expect to receive and what it is our duty to contribute. In what ways has contemporary society got the balance right, and where are there areas of concern?

9 'Blessed are those who are persecuted because of righteousness, for theirs is the kingdom of heaven. Blessed are you when people insult you, persecute you and falsely say all kinds of evil against you because of me. Rejoice and be glad, because great is your reward in heaven, for in the same way they persecuted the prophets who were before you' (Matthew 5.10–12). Persecution is a terrible thing. How can it ever bring blessing?

Chapter Seven

Doing the Right Thing in Genetics

What is genetics?

We live in a fast changing and complex society. It's sometimes hard for Christians to keep up with the big moral and ethical questions of our day. It's so easy for us to say 'this is right' or 'that's wrong' without really weighing up the arguments or testing them against what the Bible actually teaches, not in a verse here or there, but in the wholeness of its message. The scientific advances in genetic manipulation provide a prime example of a moral aspect of life that many Christians feel is too complex to tackle at all. 'Doing the right thing' is especially hard when you aren't sure you have correctly grasped the issues.

Genetics is the study of how we are made. As long ago as 1865 an Augustinian monk called Gregor Mendel suggested that there are 'laws of inheritance' from one generation to another. He based his theory on studies of pea plants in his monastery garden. Scientists continued to build on his research over the years and by 1953 Watson and Crick had identified the physical structure of these 'units of inheritance' as deoxyribonucleic acid, a nucleic acid that contains the genetic instructions used in the development and functioning of all known living organisms, popularly known as DNA.

On 26 June 2000 Frank Collins and Craig Ventor announced that they had completed a working draft of the entire human genome (map of human DNA). This breakthrough has lead to a rapid advance of the science of genetics, enabling radically new possibilities in our methods of predicting, diagnosing, preventing and treating disease.

Disease has a genetic component, and the science of genetics is working with this aspect of disease to offer new therapies able to repair the damage done to the human DNA by disease processes. Increasingly, scientific endeavour will be focused on intervention to prevent this DNA damage rather than on curing disease caused by it.

Over the last twenty years geneticists have achieved a far more profound understanding. We now know that we have about 30,000 genes that make us what we are and provide the necessary genetic information that builds our bodies.

Some geneticists believe that we must use this science now to prevent the birth of babies with genetic defects, arguing that failure to do so means that we place unnecessary burdens on the rising generation, who will be left to grapple with genetic flaws which we could so easily have engineered out of human DNA.

Geneticists also suggest that, because we have the means to increase the chances of a child being born with a healthy genetic endowment, we should use them. They indicate that our failure to do so would be both unjust and uncaring.

I accept that this argument is valid, and I don't agree with those Christians who simply say that 'all genetics is wrong'. This simplistic view is based on the same kind of prejudice that forbids blood transfusions or surgical procedures of any sort. It is not a helpful contribution to a serious moral and ethical debate, and fails to take into account that every time someone (perhaps of Japanese descent) chooses a partner (maybe of Swedish origins) and they start a family, every time a gardener chooses this plant over that, every time a Yorkshire Terrier escapes and forms a surprise alliance with a Poodle, a new genetic possibility is chosen.

Sam Berry (the Professor Emeritus in Genetics at

University College in London) and his wife Dr Caroline Berry (a genetics practitioner) have devoted much of their working lives to studies in this discipline. They have both made outstanding contributions to the field, and although retired they tirelessly advocate the work of the geneticist as a contemporary part of Christ's healing ministry.

They believe that the science of genetics can bring transformation, healing and wholeness into a broken world. Both Sam and Caroline Berry bring the highest Christian moral perspectives to their genetic science.

Sam explained to me that we have 46 chromosomes, 23 from each parent, and that these have a code which tells the chemicals in the cells what to do. He believes that we should be using this knowledge that God has given us to understand how these chromosomes can be used to further the healing of humanity.

A huge number of ordinary diseases have a genetic component, and as we begin to understand more about their genetic causes we can make advances to eradicate them.

Sam is a real enthusiast. He has travelled all over the world, studying genetic phenomena in some of the most isolated places on earth. He has an ability to make this complex subject sound understandable as well as fascinating. He feels frustrated that so many Christians are prejudiced against the wise handling of scientific advances in genetics, and he recently told me that 'if swapping the odd gene can bring healing and wholeness to the world then it should be done without hesitation!'

Caroline, his wife, is a genetic counsellor. She has been at the sharp end of the practice of genetics, and has had the delicate task of applying this science to patient care in the consulting room. Caroline went into genetics thinking that she could drop out if she did not agree with what she learnt. She soon realised, however, that this was a field in which her Christian conscience and voice were really needed. She hopes that more and more young scientists who are committed Christians will involve themselves in this work, and so offer to its ethical debate voices informed by prayer and faith as well as education and training. She told me of different cases in which this science has brought transformation and hope into very difficult medical situations.

The rapidly evolving science of genetics brings exciting possibilities that offer hope of improved health and well being for many. But real concerns arise from some areas connected with the practice of this science, that Christians cannot afford to ignore. Three of these areas of concern are the use of embryos in experimentation and treatment; the copyrighting of DNA for commercial purposes; and the use of genetics in ante-natal testing and in the potential future production of 'designer babies.'

Who is accountable to whom?

Who, then, should police this new science and to whom should scientists make themselves accountable? Some argue that only scientists who are directly involved in this field have the knowledge and expertise to understand the complex moral dilemmas that are involved. Others point out that, precisely because they are so focused on their subject, they will not have the impartiality to take a step back and review the wider ethical implications of the whole field.

Some feel that genetic practice should remain within the oversight of government departments, who have sufficient resources to oversee and control what is being done. But the rapid development of the field of genetics inevitably attracts considerable funding by the pharmaceutical industry, whose big players have huge commercial interest in the advances made. Global corporations can easily evade the legal scrutiny of one government by moving their laboratories to another country where there is a more flexible attitude to legal safeguards.

Governments are not infallible, either, and certainly not

without bias in assessing appropriate courses of action. Some politicians see the commercial possibilities of this new science, and would prefer that these new technologies remain within their own economy rather than going elsewhere, even if this means relaxing legal constrictions. Some have questioned the British government's motives in hesitating to intervene in the genetic experiments currently under way at Newcastle University, concerning what have been called 'mitochondrial transplants' – the first step towards genetically engineered babies.

Lee Silver, a professor of molecular biology at Princeton University, has written 'For better or worse, a new age is upon us – an age in which we as humans will gain the ability to change the nature of our species.' In this new situation it's crucial that Christians discern where the skills of geneticists are being used for the purposes of God or for the destruction of what God has made. They must ask which aspects of this science are to be welcomed, which are to be spurned, and where it is necessary to proceed with wise caution.

I'm convinced that this is such a sensitive area, with such massive implications for the future of the human race, that there needs to be tight control of its development. Sadly, the pressures of self interest are likely to spoil effective control by any one group, be they research scientists, physicians, parents, or funding bodies such as pharmaceutical giants.

Some years ago the British government appointed a committee under the chairmanship of Dame Mary Warnock DBE to investigate this blossoming new science. The committee reported to Parliament in 1984, and the centrepiece of its recommendations was the creation of a statutory licensing authority to regulate all research and treatment which involved the use of IVF embryos. This authority was formed in 1990 and was called the Human Fertilisation and Embryology Authority (HFEA).

The Warnock Committee recommended that: 'The Authority should be specifically charged with the responsibility to regulate and monitor practice in relation to those sensitive areas which raise fundamental ethical questions.' It's important that Christians keep informed about the work of this Authority, and play their part in ensuring that it continues to fulfil its legal obligations.

The members of the HFEA are appointed by the Secretary of State and it cannot have a medical practitioner or a scientist engaged in IVF treatment or research as its chairman or deputy chairman. The majority of its members must be lay people without scientific or medical qualifications. Its membership must be drawn from a broad range of backgrounds such as the social, legal, managerial, religious and philosophical disciplines, as well as some members with medical and scientific experience. The HFEA model is an example of good practice in its scrupulous efforts to arrive at a balanced view, though it still has the drawback of channelling major decisions about genetics through a think-tank which could be seen to be professionally and socially elitist.

As we have seen from the short history of the HFEA, there can be areas of weakness in the deliberations of such a panel of experts. Diversity of approach, attitude and rationale is inevitably limited by selection from a narrow band of the population, and this must be balanced against the clear advantage of bringing highly educated, trained professional minds to the delicate and vital task of ethical assessment.

I would like to see a more rigorous process in the workings of the HFEA which integrates moral and religious perspectives with the insights of politicians and lawyers. I would be much more comfortable with a process of giving permission to geneticists that was not top-down, but focused in a much longer and more in-depth consultative process at different levels of society. If we focus the power to permit genetic experimentation into too few hands, the risks are magnified.

If we look at how legislatures have failed to protect the environment over recent generations we can see just how unfocused and ineffective they can be, and how susceptible to commercial interests and pressures. If the same laissez-faire attitude applies to genetics the interests of commercial advantage could become the real genetic engineers of the years to come.

The urgency with which some scientists want to pursue the project of genetic manipulation seems incautious and careless of risk. Genetics holds the possibility of doing much good, but this science also has the potential for human destruction on a massive scale.

The decisions which we make today will have lasting implications for future generations. Biotechnological advance is accelerating. Today's scientific breakthroughs will affect all future generations for good or ill. It is therefore unthinkable that such crucial courses of action be decided and implemented without the input at every stage of Christian critique and prayer support. The debate is complex and at times technical, the ethical issues complicated by the reality that much of the time we are estimating outcomes still unknown. Many Christians, finding the scientific material daunting and the moral issues unnervingly difficult, are discouraged from any participation in this adventure at all, neither investigating the matters under discussion nor thinking and praying through to an opinion of their own. Many, regarding themselves as utterly incompetent to assess the matters at issue, leave everything to the Human Fertilisation and Embryology Authority to sort out. Yet the reality is, the body of Christ is called by God to a prophetic ministry. If we are Christians, then whether we like it or not we have a prophetic responsibility. Choosing to opt out of the prophetic dimension of our calling is not a possibility available to us. It is incumbent upon us to educate and inform ourselves so that we can be faithful in bringing apposite Christian insight to the issues affecting our age. Not every individual Christian is called to become a top-flight geneticist; it is the church as a whole, as a body, that must offer prophetic response – but we owe it to ourselves, to God, and to our community, at least to have enquired, thought and prayed.

Embryo research

The controversy about embryo research centres on the status of the fertilised embryo, and the complex debate about where an individual human life begins. Some say that a human life doesn't start until well after birth, and certainly not until a baby or young child reaches a level of conscious awareness and thought.

Others draw the line at the point of birth, and with their limited scientific understanding Augustine and Aquinas would have drawn the line here. Some, particularly in the medical profession, believe that we become human beings before birth, and can be considered as human individuals from that point at which life becomes viable. Today, this is normally considered to be after the first 28 weeks of pregnancy, though some babies born before that age survive.

New techniques of photography which have made it possible for us to film the developing foetus in the womb have affected public opinion, however, and many now feel that individual life begins when the foetus starts to move.

Even more recent research has detected brain activity in the foetus at six weeks; so some now argue that this indicates the potential for consciousness at this early stage, and they draw the line for individual human existence here.

Another school of thought adopts the principle that everything is in place for human development the moment the embryo attaches to the wall of the mother's uterus and implantation occurs. This is the point, they say, at which human existence becomes a real possibility.

The philosopher Aristotle, however, would have drawn the line of human existence at the moment of fertilisation itself. The more I consider the alternatives outlined above, the more I agree with Aristotle and the more concerned I become about the moveable line of human life.

I fear that, as soon as we move the line beyond the instant of fertilisation, we fail to recognise the unique and immeasurable value of human life. I'm with Aristotle, and that's why I consider the fertilised embryo to be sacrosanct.

The embryo is a highly sophisticated structure. Even in the single cell state it contains a genetic code of instructions involving three billion pairs of chemicals! From the very beginning of our lives, with the fertilised embryo, the code of our life was in place to influence our characteristics, traits and tendencies. This embryo is a self-developing living entity, it has a full human genetic code and should therefore be considered as a human being in every detail of potential. The early stage, when we see no more than a blob of human tissue – a speck of human 'stuff' – is surely the time when this human life relies upon us utterly for protection: we are not to conclude that unrealised potential is a valid excuse to throw a life away.

Personally, I am convinced that when we tamper with the human embryo we tamper with God's template for humankind. We trespass into an area that is at the core of human existence and dabble with the very stuff that makes us human.

I believe that the fertilised human egg should be sacrosanct. I fear that increasing use of the embryo for research or treatment opens us up to a world of horrific possibilities that has scant regard for the essence of human life.

At the very beginning of the Christian story is the account of Mary's visit from an angel who told her, 'Thou shalt conceive and bring forth a son.' This moment of conception was the holy moment in which divinity and humanity were fused and the incarnation became reality. Mary went to see her cousin Elizabeth immediately, and it's clear that the person of Jesus is already present even in that earliest stage of embryonic development. Elizabeth's baby leaps in her womb at this encounter with the newly conceived Jesus. 'The mother of my Lord', is how Elizabeth describes Mary. The development of the foetus, the baby, the child, the man, the ascended one, all are stages in the revelation of who, from before time began, He was.

In Genesis chapters 1 and 9 we read that the human race was created in God's image, and that human life is not to be taken away unjustly. I believe that human embryos are created in God's image, and are therefore sacrosanct. Psalm 139 points out that there is no place to hide from God, even in the unformed body of the foetus in the womb.

The HFEA states in its own papers that its 'power in section 3(1), makes it a criminal offence to bring about the creation of an embryo or keep or use an embryo except pursuant to a licence from the authority.' It is disappointing and disturbing that this body in its power to grant such licences has sometimes crossed what seemed to be the boundaries of wise caution and ethical restraint.

Britain became the first Western nation to give scientists the right to clone human embryos for medical research. The decision was made by the HFEA, and it gave a team at Newcastle on Tyne University an initial one year licence to use the 'cell nuclear transfer technique' which was first used in 1996 to clone Dolly the sheep.

Skin cells were taken from women and their nuclei transferred into eggs from which genetic material had been removed. The resultant cloned 'human embryos' were primarily used to investigate treatments for type 1 diabetes, an illness caused by defective cells in the pancreas which do not produce enough of the hormone insulin.

Some scientists hoped that this research could lead to a medical breakthrough which meant that laboratory-grown embryos could be used extensively in the treatment of diabetes. A patient's cells would be used to clone an embryo, and then embryonic stem cells would be harvested for their own personal treatment. Because these cells came from the patient's own compatible source, the body would not reject the harvested cells.

Christians generally have two significant concerns about this kind of frontier research. Firstly, it involves the destruction of human embryos. Those of us who consider the human embryo to be an integral part of God's sacred gift of life feel that the scientists are destroying something sacred, even though it is being used for a worthy cause.

Helen Watt, the director of the Linacre Centre for Healthcare Ethics, said: 'Therapeutic cloning creates a human life in exactly the same way as reproductive cloning does. The only difference is that the embryo is not intended for birth but for laboratory destruction.' I struggle with such a concept, even if it is being done with the highest intentions for the prevention of human disease.

The second area of concern is that this research can only advance the scientific possibility of producing the first cloned human baby. The techniques involved are identical to those needed for such a procedure, and we should have deep reservations about the development of such a scientific process. Once invented, like the atomic bomb, it will be a process almost impossible to keep under control.

Catholic ethicist Richard Doerflinger describes reproductive techniques such as this as essentially dehumanizing. He writes: 'There's something about these processes that seems to invite researchers, especially, to see the product of these processes as uniquely subhuman.'

I am grateful that in 2001 President Bush outlawed the use of US federal funds for embryonic stem cell research for this very reason. He has been harshly criticised by many in the British media for doing so.

It would be wrong to say that all Christians share my concerns. Some of my Christian friends argue that God has given us this understanding of DNA for the purpose of eradicating such terrible diseases as diabetes, Alzheimer's, obesity, epilepsy, blindness, high blood pressure, osteoporosis, melanoma, growth hormone disorders, arthritis, breast and ovarian cancer, cardiovascular disease and Parkinson's disease.

One spokesman for this view is Lawrence Goldstein, a stem cell expert from the University of California, who claims that 'research could bring benefits for patients in a minimum of two years and a maximum of twenty years.' Those who share his perspective look to a world where the genetic component implicated in all of these illnesses will be corrected, using the kind of technologies which the Newcastle team are exploring. They argue that this medical development contributes to healing and wholeness, which are part of the Christian vision for the world, and that we should be encouraging this research, not standing in its way.

Yet my conscience is uneasy when I consider the ever increasing use of human embryos in this kind of genetic research. I believe that the human embryo is sacred, and makes up part of the bundle of life at the core of human existence. I feel a desire deep down to see legislation in which embryos are protected from harm, and never harvested for experimentation. And yet I am embarrassed to be categorised as an unsophisticated reactionary completely out of touch with current scientific thinking, an intellectual dinosaur trapped by religious superstition. I fear that one day, however, my hesitation, the instinct to draw back from this scientific frontier, shared by many Christians, will come to be seen as a prophetic voice 'crying in the wilderness' – but by then it will be too late to put this sinister genie back in the bottle.

I suspect that creating human embryos for destruction is not so much necessary as scientifically expedient, and I believe the use of adult stem cells should be normative for research. Adult stem cell experimentation has led to a large number of successful medical treatments, and many thousands of adult stem cell therapies are carried out annually around the world.

There are scientific difficulties in using embryonic cells. They are less specific in their function than adult cells and are much more likely to cause unwanted growth along with desirable growth. When adult cells from the patient's own body are used there is much less likelihood of rejection than if embryonic cells using a different genetic code are used.

Recent studies show that adult stem cells in the bone marrow can be used to produce any type of cell found in the body, and that stem cells from spinal fluid are flexible enough to produce tissue for vital organs such as the liver.

Proverbs 31:8 calls on us to 'Speak up for those who cannot speak for themselves.' It's tragic to think that one of the riskiest places on earth for human life is the fertilised human embryo. In the miracle of conception God has created a soul in His image, and I believe that the spark of the human spirit exists from this moment of conception. If we lose our hold on the value of that, we've lost the basic understanding of what it is that beautifies and enobles humanity; the wise compassion that protects the vulnerable and weak.

The Hashmi case

One of my heroes in the ethics of genetics is Josephine Quintavalle, the founder of Comment on Reproductive Ethics, an organisation which monitors the work of the HFEA. She has, with very limited resources and often little support from the churches, carefully scrutinised the practices of the HFEA since its inception. Where necessary she has gone to law to question some of its different rulings.

Josephine often appears on national television news bulletins whenever issues involving bio-ethics hit the headlines. Recently, over breakfast after appearing on my radio show, she told me of the immense personal cost of her work.

When someone like Josephine takes on the scientific establishment, with very little backing, it demands a commitment and resourcefulness of heroic proportions. One of her most important cases involved the HFEA's permission given for embryo selection in the well documented case of Mrs Hashmi.

The case first arose because Mrs Hashmi's son Zain, four years old, was diagnosed with the genetic disorder beta thalassemia. The submission to the HFEA was that Zain's chance of survival would be maximised if his parents, with the aid of in-vitro fertilisation, could produce a 'compatible embryo'. The resulting baby could then provide suitable transplant treatment to cure Zain's condition. Mrs Hashmi hoped to produce a 'saviour sibling', as the popular press called it.

The ethical argument around this case centred on the number of viable embryos which would have to be produced in order to find a suitable one for the purpose of Zain's treatment. All the embryos except the selected one would be destroyed.

The Court of Appeal gave permission for the Hashmi family to have a child by in-vitro fertilisation in order to provide a 'life-saving' bone marrow transplant for Zain. This ruling overturned a December 2002 High Court judgment in favour of Josephine's organisation Comment on Reproductive Ethics (CORE), who argued that granting a licence for the search for and selection of a 'suitable' (i.e. healthy and free of defects, genetically matching) embryo set a precedent for the creation of designer babies. The appeal was widely applauded in the press, and in particular by the HFEA and the British Medical Association (BMA).

For the Hashmi family, only about one in five embryos produced by IVF would offer the right HLA tissue type and be free of the disease. In addition, in a woman of Mrs Hashmi's age, the chance of any implanted embryo surviving was around 10 percent per cycle (with each cycle costing around £2,500).

So around 50 embryos would need to be discarded or lost for each one that survived. Even then there would be difficulties with prenatal screening. Zain himself initially tested normal, and an earlier sibling who was thought to be a good match turned out not to be. Another sibling was aborted when found to have Zain's condition. For a successful treatment hundreds of embryos might need to be discarded.

The hurry to conceive a sibling was not because Zain was about to die, though he required monthly blood transfusions and drip-fed drugs to control his symptoms, but because his mother, Shahana, was 39 years old and an IVF child would not remain an option for long.

Peter Saunders, of the Christian Medical Fellowship, has pointed out that 'hard cases make bad law' and the Hashmi ruling created a very dangerous precedent. He wrote: 'Many of us already have severe misgivings about pre-implantation diagnosis, a procedure already legal in this country, whereby human embryos having various disabilities are searched out and destroyed. This seems to strike at the very heart of Christian morality, which decrees that the strong have a duty to protect and respect the weak. It also runs counter to the Declaration of Geneva (1948), which calls doctors to "maintain the utmost respect for human life from the time of conception against threat". After all, what human life is more vulnerable and defenceless than an embryo with special needs?'

The Hashmi ruling opened the door for human beings to be manufactured for the primary purpose of providing tissue for someone else. It is particularly disturbing that the proposed treatment involved significant mortality of human embryos where the chances of success were quite low.

Nothing is as simple as it seems, for it also appears that research scientists have used this highly emotive case to legitimise the controversial practice of embryo selection for tissue type.

Though Josephine Quintavalle's opposition to the treatment was parodied in the popular press, who heralded the

Appeal Court ruling as a victory for common sense, there was much more to the story than they reported.

Newspaper reports about the saviour sibling being 'Zain's only chance for survival' were both emotive and inaccurate. Specialists tell me that a treatment programme of regular monthly transfusions and chelation therapy makes it possible for patients with the disease to survive for 40 or 50 years and that results are improving all the time.

Descriptions of what the 'saviour sibling' could do for Zain were also exaggerated. Bone marrow transplantation from a tissue-matched donor (almost always a sibling) for both conditions offers the only chance of a complete cure, but there are major risks.

Some 5 percent of patients do not survive the procedure, and a further 10 percent are not cured; and there are also the long-term risks of debilitating 'graft versus host disease' and the side-effects of immuno-suppressant drugs, which include increased susceptibility to infection and some forms of cancer.

The manipulation of public opinion by journalists in this case is very disquieting. The impression given by the media was that Zain Hashmi would die without the transplant and that such a transplant would be straightforward and uncomplicated. This was quite misleading. Public opinion is a powerful factor in this debate, and it's crucial that Christians delve further into the subject than the banner headlines of the popular press.

Josephine's legal argument in this case focused on 'suitable' and 'viable'. 'Suitable' is one of those adjectives which leaves its meaning to be determined entirely by context. To quote from the legal papers delivered in the House of Lords, Josephine's legal counsel pointed out that the word 'suitable':

> would enable the authority to authorise a single cell biopsy to test the embryo for whatever characteristics the mother might wish to know: whether the child would be male or female, dark or blonde, perhaps even, in time to come, intelligent or stupid.

Suitable must therefore have a narrower meaning than suitable for that particular mother.

We should be deeply grateful that people like Josephine are painstaking and aware enough to discern the implication of terms such as 'suitable' and 'viable'. The safeguards which are put in place at the start of a legislative process are often eroded over the years, and can be undermined in legal argument when the public mind is not alert to underlying implications of the argument. Unless Christians are willing to devote time and resources to the ethical considerations of genetics, much moral ground will be lost in just the same way as has happened with abortion.

The effects of the science of genetics are so far reaching that much is at stake that is not always immediately apparent. Christians must take responsibility to inform themselves about scientific development and government legislation, and the interpretation of that by authorising bodies. We must exercise our influence in the communities we serve, the governments we elect and the authorities who represent us. As 'salt and light' in the arcane enviroment of scientific research we must not evade the responsibility to engage in debate just because we have to work hard to fully grasp the issues. Each of us must seek God, and speak out.

Pre-natal testing

If truth be known, everyone would like a 'perfect baby'. The range of opinions as to what a 'perfect baby' might be like is probably too numerous to quantify! Some would simply see a perfect baby as one that is fit and healthy, but other couples would see their perfect baby as being of a specific sex, hair or eye colour, sexual orientation, or level of intelligence.

As the science of genetics gets more advanced, the moral and ethical issues raised by the choices it gives to parents will become more and more complicated. Many of those choices are not with us yet, or are not legally permitted. Yet, even now, pre-natal testing can cause mind-bending moral and ethical dilemmas.

Many of the parents who go for pre-natal testing have already faced major tragedies in their lives. They may have had a child who has died from a debilitating illness, or have other children who are severely disabled. They often feel that they simply couldn't cope with another child in a similar situation. They are not looking for a 'designer' baby with blue eyes and blonde hair; they just want a healthy child!

Dr John Wyatt, the Professor of Neo-natal Science at University College Hospital in London, told me that medical technology already enables us to diagnose many foetal problems and that as the science advances we will be able to detect more and more minor abnormalities.

In his clinical experience, some parents are able to accept that their child may not be completely normal whilst others regard it as their natural right to have a perfectly healthy child. Some have very real fears about their own ability to cope with a physically impaired baby, and others seem desperate to have a 'perfect' child.

John has observed that there often seems little appreciation that those who overcome disabilities and hardships may contribute the most to society and develop the greatest personalities. Their contribution to the community may be the outstanding feature of their lives, rather than the disabilities that emerged as the significant factor initially.

At present, genetic counselling and pre-natal testing are frequently used to offer parents the choice of a termination of pregnancy where there has been a diagnosis of hereditary disease such as muscular dystrophy, cystic fibrosis and Huntington's disease. In the future, this may well be extended to cover many more medical problems, and as this science grows it seems likely that more and more parents will choose to abort.

Sharon Anson, the founder of a mission agency called

Grassroots, offers an interesting personal illustration of what this practice actually meant for her as an expectant mother. Following a difficult illness in her first child, she was offered pre-natal testing in her next pregnancy to determine the health of her baby.

She told me that she decided to have the tests because, as a 'control freak', she wanted to have some kind of idea of what she and her husband Hugo were facing. The results led to pressure from the midwife to choose termination of the pregnancy. Sharon was amazed and angered by the natural assumption that because the tests had suggested the presence of clinical problems, it was assumed that she would naturally want to abort the baby. Sharon felt that the readiness to counsel termination implied that the precious new life that she was carrying was regarded as cheap and dispensable. She chose to keep her baby, and the tests turned out to be inaccurate. Sharon's baby was born without the illness that the medical professionals had predicted, and on the basis of which they had recommended termination.

When parents are informed that their child might have a serious physical or mental impairment the resulting fear and shock can be overwhelming. They frequently experience strong emotions, and feel they cannot cope with the practical implications of caring for a severely disabled child for the rest of their lives.

Down's syndrome is a case in point. The numbers of Down's syndrome children in the community have fallen dramatically over recent years because we now destroy many of the embryos which test positive for this. I see this as a designing-out of those who don't conform to our standards of perfection. This clinical approach is a continuum that begins as therapeutic support of human communities, families and individuals, but arrives through a series of confusing decisions at the end-point of first genetic, then social engineering. Brave new world.

A crucial principle of Christian medical ethics is that we

cannot define the value of human beings in terms of the 'bundle of faculties' they possess. Human beings must always be valued because they represent the gift of life which God has given. Our humanity rests on our relationship with the Creator, and God's perfect and endless love for His children – no matter what their mental or physical condition. Once we move away from this basic understanding of human life, we take a seismic shift from the Judaeo-Christian principles which underpin our civilisation.

This process of genetic diagnosis, with its intention to weed out disabilities from the community by ending the lives of unborn disabled children, is being taken a stage too far. Implicit in this practice is the unspoken concept that a person born with disabilities is somehow less valuable than others. It is inherently political and social in its judgments, because the stark reality beneath the talk about 'testing to see the baby is okay' and 'picking up problems' or 'weeding out illnesses' is the implication that it is undesirable for a disabled person to be born at all.

Legally, genetic testing allows us to abort for 'severe disability', but as the term 'severe' is relative and open to interpretation, it can lead to decisions to abort because of repairable defects such as a cleft palate (as described in the chapter on abortion).

Geneticists have an important role in counselling parents about the likelihood of hereditary disease being passed on through their genes, advising them of the risks that they take in conceiving a child with their particular genetic make up, offering advice as to how best to evaluate the risks and optimise their chances of conceiving a healthy baby. This seems to be a reasonable and responsible approach to clinical prevention of the occurrence of disability. Some hereditary illnesses are terrible to bear, and put significant pressure on every member of a family. The decision to forgo parenthood can be the preferred option in that circumstance for some couples; but in moral terms, it is a different choice from the option of inviting a new life to begin, but permitting it to continue only if tests suggest the child to be free of disease.

Pre-natal testing can put pressure on a woman and her partner to choose termination when their unborn child is diagnosed as having a physical or mental impairment. The judgment of the medical experts involved can, knowingly or unknowingly, indicate that an abortion might be in everyone's interests and in some way make it morally justifiable.

Pre-natal screening can easily convey the wrong message about disability. It can communicate to society as a whole that disability of any kind is unwelcome in our world and that the embryo is some kind of easily disposable 'stuff'. After an embryo has tested positive for a clinical condition the unspoken implication is that it should be thrown away and the process repeated until a healthy embryo becomes available. This escalates into a ruthless process of human destruction.

Knowledge opens the door of opportunity, and opportunity becomes duty, and duty becomes inevitability – step by step the moral thresholds are crossed, and so it has been in the case of genetics.

This runaway science, if unchecked, will generate an unstoppable demand for parents to choose the sex, hair and eye colour, and intelligence level of their offspring. In turn this will lead to the destruction of human embryos on a massive scale, with scores being discarded until the perfect one is created. It's a possibility which I find completely abhorrent and which will ultimately fulfil the darkest nightmares of science fiction.

The further down this road that we travel, the nearer we get to children being seen as commodities created to order, rather than beings of idiosyncrasy and full of surprises, received with gratitude as a gift from God, just as they are.

A voice for the voiceless

Josephine Quintavalle sees herself as a defender of the right to life of the embryo. She thinks that, as Christians, we have a duty to bear witness to God's creation and to teach the highest level of respect for the life of the embryo.

I stand with her. I believe that as Christians we must influence and shape society, and discover what is God's perfect will. If we don't take this responsibility seriously, I fear that commercial or political forces will use this science for their own purposes, without regard for the sacred mystery in every human life.

Our Christian faith is more than just singing hymns and saying prayers. It is not only personal and private, but has a moral and political dimension, a prophetic task in shaping the society of which we are part. We have a responsibility, not only for what we do as individuals, but for what is done in our name by governments and research scientists.

Christians must learn how to ask the right questions, examine the ethical standards, speak up for the truth and bear witness to Christ in the complex sphere of genetics. Our future society will be shaped not only by what we do, but also by what we ignore or leave undone; and God, who called us to faith, will also require an account of how we put our faith to work.

The urgent need now is not immediately for more scientific knowledge and research, but for a wise consensus in determining ethical and moral guidelines to make best use of the sciencific advances we have already made. If scientific progress continues apace without such guidelines, we will end up with a world in which human life is devalued, human relationships are cheapened and the quality of life eroded.

The science of genetics can bring healing and hope to the world, and if geneticists work with the grain of God's moral law they can do much good. If, however, science is simply driven by greed and financial gain, or the rationale that because we can do it, we must – then this new knowledge has the potential to damage countless millions of people and undermine the basis of society on a grand scale. Already the copyrighting of DNA is taking place with governmental permission. What God has given as the template of human life is already being used for business and profit.

May God give geneticists and governments wisdom! For as scientists handle the very stuff of life, they handle the sacred. That which has the potential of human life is a gift from God and must be considered as holy. It must be handled with care.

John Stott once wrote: 'God has given us the Bible and its witness to Christ in order to direct and control our thinking … as we absorb its teaching, our thoughts will increasingly conform to His.' We urgently need Christians who are theologically literate and have scientific understanding to bring some much needed wisdom into the developing field of genetics.

Discussion Questions

1 What do you understand about the science of genetics, and what do you feel about its contribution to modern society?

2 If modifying or substituting a gene can bring help to sick people with chronic conditions, what boundaries should be set to gene therapy?

3 'For better or worse, a new age is upon us – an age in which we as humans will gain the ability to change the nature of our species.' How does this assertion make you feel?

4 By what means do you think the powers of genetic manipulation might best be regulated? Who would you choose to be on a panel authorised to give permission for genetic intervention, and what would be the reasons for your choice?

5 The philosopher Aristotle believed a human life began at the moment of fertilisation itself. At what point do you think life begins?

6 'The human embryo is sacred, and makes up part of the 'stuff' which is at the core of human existence.' Do you agree or disagree? What kind of legislation to protect embryos would you like to see?

7 Mary went to see her cousin Elizabeth immediately, and it's clear that the person of Jesus is already present as just an embryo. Elizabeth's baby leaps in her womb at this encounter with the newly conceived Jesus! Why is this story important to this subject?

8 Genetic counselling and pre-natal testing are frequently used to give parents choices about the avoidance of hereditary diseases such as muscular dystrophy, cystic fibrosis and Huntington's disease. In the future, this may well be extended to cover many more medical problems, and as this science grows it seems likely that more and more parents will choose to abort. What do you feel about this?

9 Human beings must always be valued because they represent the gift of life which God has given. Their humanity rests on

their relationship with the Creator, and God's perfect and endless love for His children – no matter what their physical or
mental state. Why is this concept so important?

Chapter Eight

Doing the Right Thing by the Unborn

The mystery of life

Two of the most difficult and traumatic experiences in my marriage occurred on the occasions when my wife Jacqui miscarried. In both situations we came to a powerful recognition of the mystery and reality of human life in the womb, and shared a deep sense of personal loss for an unborn human being.

On the seemingly endless drive in the back of an ambulance from our holiday house in Felixstowe to the massive new hospital in Ipswich, the blue lights stabbed the night air and the siren wailed. We sped through dark Suffolk villages hoping beyond hope that we could save the unborn baby.

I will never forget being called into that bright neon-lighted Accident and Emergency consulting room to see jacqui in tears, and to hear that the foetus would need to be aborted immediately. Nor will I ever forget her return from surgery to a darkened ward, and holding hands, both of us numb with shock, and overwhelmed by the great mysteries of life and death.

It is impossible for me to accept that a foetus is a disposable 'it' and not a real human being. Our two experiences of miscarriage reinforced that understanding, and to us the loss of both our unborn children was a very real tragedy. It was made all the more painful because, on both occasions, my wife was accommodated in a ward full of patients awaiting abortions.

Pastoral situations involving women seeking abortion have not been a feature of my ministry, so I can only speculate about the potential emotional, physical and psychological after-effects; but the evidence I have come across suggests that abortion does have long term consequences for many women. From my own very personal experiences of witnessing miscarriage in my own marriage, I can't help but feel that this must be true.

Admittedly, a termination often signals some kind of personal tragedy or desperate situation. There may well be a sense of overwhelming relief when the operation is over; but few, if any, would see such a destruction of life as a cause for celebration.

The moral questions

The key aspect of this debate must be the question: where does life begin? Your answer to this question is bound to shape your overall view of abortion, and there are many long and complex arguments about the moment when life begins. Eminent theologians, philosophers and lawyers have tried to make a case that it begins at conception or at any specified number of weeks up to the moment of birth itself.

The Bible speaks of the unborn child as a person loved by God and to whom God relates. If, as many Christians believe, life begins at conception, then the foetus shares our human rights. This cluster of cells is not merely just a part of its mother, but an unborn child with a life of its own.

In Jeremiah 1:5 we read: 'Before I formed you in the womb I knew you.' And that wonderful passage in Psalm 139 reminds us that: 'Thou didst form my inward parts, Thou didst knit me together in my mother's womb, Thou knowest me right well ... my frame was not hidden from Thee when I was being made in secret.'

I believe that human life begins at conception. In that instant all the potential for human existence comes together, and so the act of terminating a pregnancy must therefore result in the ending of a human life. From my understanding of the Bible, such a procedure would be very hard for Christians to justify. Because I believe that human life begins at conception I just can't accept that one person has the right to deny another the right to live.

I disagree with those who believe that one stage of foetal development is more significant than another. This view sets dangerous precedents. If a foetus of twelve weeks has less value than a baby at birth, then why shouldn't a newborn have less value than a four-year-old? The intellectual flow of such an argument can quickly lead us to the abhorrent practice of infanticide.

Many, of course, don't even consider where life begins, believing that termination of pregnancy is nothing more than the exercise of a woman's rights over her own body. They see a woman's choice as paramount, and any questioning of her rights as inadmissible.

This argument is fundamentally flawed. The life growing within her is not part of her body. It has a life separate from her own. When you look at an ultrasound picture and see the beating heart of a foetus; it's clear that a woman's choice to abort will deny the right to life for another separate life. The same gynaecological and maternity unit that offers termination of pregnancy up to six weeks may also offer to fight for the life of a baby that has come early, perhaps at 26 weeks or even as early as 22 weeks.

I believe that life is a gift from God, so I can't accept that we can choose to destroy it. A woman's 'right to choose' means choosing to destroy a life that is not her own.

Many Christians find it difficult to accept that abortion is wrong in every case, arguing that the issues to be weighed are very complex. Some Christians, though they may not be in favour of abortion, distance themselves from the pro-life movement because they perceive its advocates as interfering in very personal decisions and lacking in compassion for women in very difficult circumstances. Yet anti-abortion activists were often drawn into the pro-life movement because they have witnessed first-hand a close friend going through the trauma of post-abortion distress, or have had an abortion themselves but lived to regret it. Many pro-life campaigners are not the judgmental people they are caricatured as being, but are in fact full of compassion for women who have had abortions. Many are sad that so many pregnant women have been taken in by spurious arguments that human life does not begin until birth, or that a woman's rights are the only thing to be considered; and outraged by the pressure that is put on women to accept abortion as an apparently simple and necessary solution to a difficult life situation.

The Abortion Act

Future generations will look back with incredulity and disgust at what has taken place in the UK over the last forty years. I feel a sense of shame and responsibility for what has happened in my home country during my own lifetime. And as I look back down the years I am embarrassed at my own lack of concern to have done anything about it.

The 1960s were an era of massive social change. Many deeply held convictions were challenged by the rising generation. The beginnings of the women's movement, effective birth control and the growth of sexual liberation caused many to feel that it was time to legalise abortion under strict government control. The clinical dangers of back-street abortions added weight to the force of these considerations. Pro-choice campaigners successfully argued that this was no more than according women their human rights.

I was 17 years of age when the Abortion Act was first introduced, and I can still remember the persuasive arguments put forward at the time. David Steel MP and others convinced Parliament that this modernising legislation would remove the need for women to seek help from illegal back-street abortionists. The Abortion Act would give women their basic right of choice. I recall how logical and convincing were the arguments they put forward at the time.

In the year following the Abortion Act there were 800 legal abortions, and I can still remember the shock and concern expressed by Christian campaigners at the time. However, within twelve months the figure had quadrupled and has been steadily rising ever since.

Since the 1967 Abortion Act a total of 6,231,033 unborn babies have been terminated – a staggering 10 percent of the entire UK population. This is six times the number of combined UK casualties in both World Wars. More than 600 abortions take place in the UK every day, and every year more than 3,000 are terminated after more than twenty weeks in the womb. This can't be acceptable in a civilised society.

The passing of the Abortion Act crossed a moral threshold. It reshaped our understanding of life's priceless value and significantly blunted our moral sensibility.

In my research for this chapter I felt that it was important to talk to some articulate women with strong views on the subject. These included a barrister, a pro-life campaigner, a pro-choice counsellor, a politician and a vicar. These conversations convinced me even more that the Abortion Act turned the unthinkable into the commonplace.

I believe that legal abortion has been made socially acceptable by dehumanising the foetus. We have been misled into thinking that the foetus is not a real being and that abortion is not ultimately about the destruction of an actual human life.

Abortion as contraception?

Some say that abortion is the best option for an unwanted pregnancy. They argue that if a woman simply forgot to take her pill she should not be forced to bear a child against her will. While this may sound reasonable, the logic of this argument leads to abortion being seen as nothing more than just another form of contraception.

Even those organisations which have traditionally advocated a woman's 'choice' seem concerned at the increasing numbers of women seeking abortion. The nine UK clinics run by Marie Stopes International were responsible for 5,992 terminations in January 2006, a rise of 13 percent over the previous year – more than at any time in the charity's 32 year history. Liz Davies, the Marie Stopes Director of UK Operations, concluded:

> Despite our efforts we have still seen the biggest rise ever in abortion figures in the month after Christmas. We may be seeing the consequences of the festive season, when partying excess and alcohol consumption combine to increase libido and lower inhibition, with the inevitable consequences of unprotected sex resulting in unplanned pregnancies.

A spokesman for the Department of Health said that improving access to emergency contraception was 'only one part of a complex picture' in reducing abortion rates. The spokesman continued: 'Our policy has always been that safe sex, using reliable contraception on a regular basis, is the best way for women to protect against unintended pregnancy. We are working hard to reduce the demand for abortions and have undertaken an audit to identify gaps in service provision.'

The Society for the Protection of Unborn Children responded to this statement by declaring that easier access to birth control drugs and devices was not the solution, because the introduction of such measures had already failed to contain the rising number of abortions. According to Department of Health statistics, a total of 186,416 abortions were carried out in England and Wales in 2005. A total of 84 percent of these were funded by the National Health Service and over half of these were performed under contract in the independent sector by clinics such as those run by Marie Stopes and the British Pregnancy Advisory Service. Statistics for 2006 showed a further rise of 3.9 percent to a total of 193,700, of which 87 percent were funded by the NHS. The Royal College of Obstetricians and Gynaecologists (RCOG) report on this rise asserts that 'this now represents a major public health issue and a failure of preventive medicine'. It is really difficult to separate this subject from the discussion about sexuality and morality covered elsewhere, because these statistics do seem to indicate that using abortion as a form of contraception has become a fact of life.

Ground 'C'

When the 1967 Abortion Law was passed many of us felt it to be acceptable because the reasons for a termination were seriously regulated and the number of terminations rigorously restricted.

The legal safeguards stipulated that two doctors had to agree that an abortion would be in the 'best interests of the patient'. The pro-choice lobby argued that the section known as Ground 'C' was tightly worded enough to restrict the grounds for abortion. They argued that it could never become a procedure just used for convenience. Ground 'C' allowed abortion where:

> The continuance of the pregnancy would involve risk, greater than if the pregnancy were terminated, of injury to the physical or mental health of the pregnant woman.

History has shown that it's impossible to measure the extent of the risk to a woman's physical or mental health. But one doctor's estimate of what an unwanted pregnancy would do to a woman's mental health has turned out to be very different from that of another!

Those who interpreted the law more leniently attracted clients who were seeking a quick termination paid for by the NHS. The vagueness of Ground 'C' lead to a situation where many saw 'injury to mental health' as applying to anyone who was pregnant, but who didn't want to be.

This weak interpretation of Ground 'C' has had disturbing results. According to the 2003 Department of Health Statistics, a staggering 94.19 percent of terminations were carried out under Ground 'C'. How could almost 95 percent of 193,700 abortions have been carried out under the terms of Ground 'C' in one year, while still conforming to the terms of the original Act?

The RCOG statement in response to the 2006 statistics would suggest that the terms outlined in the 1967 Act are not in fact adhered to in clinical practice:

> there needs to be a rethink in the way Sex and Relationship Education (SRE) is provided in the country with the aim of changing attitudes and behaviour across all ages ...

The implication here is that the underlying factors in what RCOG recognises as 'a major public health issue' are not matters of potential injury to mind or body, but increased promiscuity, a careless approach to contraception, and a blunting of moral sensibilities in relation to the prospect of carrying out an abortion.

Ann Widdecombe MP, an enthusiastic pro-life activist for many years, hoped that the 1990 Abortion Act would improve matters, but instead the government made abortion legal up until birth. When I talked with her about her commitment to the pro-life campaign, she described her role as that of being a 'voice for the voiceless'. She has been appalled by the steady growth in the numbers of abortions and asks the question 'Where is society's conscience?'

Pastoral needs

Joanna Jepson is a vicar in South London, and whilst being a committed campaigner against abortion, she recognises the pastoral needs of those considering termination of a pregnancy. She believes that Christians can often be perceived as judgmental, distant and detached, and feels that Christians should get involved in the practical care of those with unwanted pregnancies.

Joanna has herself spent time with young girls with unplanned pregnancies, trying to understand the emotional pressures, and attempting to offer support while still respecting their right of choice. Some of the girls were devastated that their future was jeopardised by an unwanted pregnancy, and needed a friend rather than a judge.

Joanna discovered that some women face complex decisions when they learn that their unborn baby has medical problems. Some simply can't face seeing their new born baby go through many difficult surgical procedures.

Some women, for instance, find the prospect of bearing a child with serious heart defects quite overwhelming. They know that this impairment might lead to the child's death during childbirth or to extensive surgery in the early months of its life. It's little wonder that they opt for a termination, possibly feeling that they are protecting their child from enduring so gruelling a regime of surgical procedures. In situations like these there is an urgent need for a friend to accompany the mother; and no situation benefits from a critic who's simply plugging a particular moral agenda.

Joanna believes that Christians must be people of compassion and understanding. She calls on Christians to be supportive of women who are facing an abortion as much as to those who have lived through that decision in the past. Women who have had an abortion have lost a child and may well be grieving. Some of them are in a wilderness experience of great personal loss, and may even be suffering from post-abortion stress syndrome.

Joanna believes that the rights of young women to continue their education, to find a career and to reach their full potential have played a powerful part in the pro-choice movement and contributed towards increasing the social acceptability of abortion. She also believes that factors such as financial hardship, social stigma, and abusive relationships have played an important part in influencing women to opt for an abortion. She believes that Christians are called to empathise with the woman's situation, and to become involved in the reality of what she may be facing.

On several occasions the Revd Jepson has officiated at the funeral of an aborted foetus after the pregnancy was terminated for medical reasons. She believes that clergy and church leaders have an important role to play in supporting parents through traumatic experiences such as these. She has witnessed the pain of parents feeling an acute sense of guilt as well as grief in this kind of situation.

Sometimes, however, Joanna has wondered whether it would not have been better for a child with medical problems to be born and for the parents to have had the opportunity to bond with the baby, and for proper palliative care to be provided until the child dies.

Christians have a pastoral responsibility to care for women seeking support before, during or after an abortion. Christ calls us to be present in and to these situations, not distant or even absent; and to be loving and never condemnatory or judgmental.

Although many women move on with their lives after an abortion, this does not always pass without disturbance. Some hallucinate or have recurrent nightmares, whilst others suffer physical consequences such as premature delivery in future pregnancies. Whatever the outcome may be, Christians must offer emotional and spiritual support whenever it's requested.

I believe that Joanna has got it right. Whilst maintaining her own strongly held views about abortion, she does not let this affect her pastoral relationship with women inside or outside the church. The woman with an unwanted pregnancy needs a friend and although we have a responsibility to point toward the different choices she has, especially with regard to adoption, we must respect her right to choose. We have no right to take the moral high ground at a time of such intense emotional pressure.

Christians must represent Jesus who is compassionate and caring, and bring to every situation his unreserved grace and forgiveness. If we fail to do this we misrepresent our Saviour, offering a pharisaical attitude to people with a desperate need for understanding and acceptance.

Ante-natal testing

Ante-natal testing is proving to be a significant factor in the growing numbers of abortions. The development of medical ultrasound equipment and the advances in genetic testing have given doctors a much greater understanding about the medical prospects for the future of an unborn child. It is now routine for mothers to be told of any abnormality in the foetus, and to be given the choice to abort if they so choose.

The abortion of an 'imperfect' foetus poses significant moral and ethical questions, extending beyond a matter of personal dilemma into areas of social and political principle, particularly into the territory of disability issues. What does abortion say about our attitudes toward people with disabilities? Of what value does it encourage them to perceive themselves to be? Is it not inherently likely to nudge popular opinion in the direction of accepting euthanasia and assisted suicide? And doesn't this belittle the contribution to society of people with disabilities, when the reality is they are as precious and as valuable as anyone else?

For Joanna Jepson this practice is not just theoretical, but immensely personal. She was born with a jaw defect, which has been fully corrected with surgery. Her brother has Down's Syndrome. She wonders whether, had they been born in a different time and to a different family, they both might have been aborted. As it was, their parents saw each of them as a gift from God, and made the necessary personal sacrifices essential to building a strong family.

Joanna questions the reasoning that makes it acceptable to choose which child is worthy of being part of your family and which one isn't. This practice ultimately makes the 'imperfect' disposable. This desire for perfection in our children is not healthy. It undermines the importance of life and questions the value of those who are mentally or physically disabled.

Joanna was shocked when she discovered that abortions were being routinely offered to mothers whose children were likely to be born with minor disabilities – even when fairly routine cosmetic surgery could correct the problem in the majority of cases. She was so incensed that she went to court to question the legality of the practice.

Today, many women bearing a child with Down's Syndrome are advised that abortion may be the best option for both them and the child. About 20 percent of terminations after a diagnostic check are Down's syndrome cases.

However, many families with Down's Syndrome children are glad they did not have an abortion. Their Down's Syndrome children have brought them a quality of joy which they would never have known without them. Our desire for perfection can fail to appreciate that the imperfect can sometimes bring us the greatest blessing.

Jane Fisher works in a pastoral role with women who have discovered that their baby has a serious medical condition. She believes that some pregnant women simply can't face the stress of a difficult medical prognosis for their child and don't have the resources to cope or the emotional support to live with this kind of uncertainty.

Over the years of my pastoral work and hospital chaplaincy I have witnessed the kind of pressures on a family which this kind of situation can bring. It's little wonder that some consider the challenge just too great to accept.

Sometimes they fear that their relationship with their partner is not strong enough to take the pressure of caring for a sick child, or they feel that their other children would not cope, or their financial situation is too precarious. Many have no experience of dealing with stressful decisions like this. Christians need to be deeply sensitive and caring in situations such as these, even if we hold very strong views about abortion. Many of us have not had to face such complicated situations in our own lives.

The conscience clause

My research into this issue has led me to become increasingly concerned about the growing pressure on medical professionals to perform abortions. The Abortion Act provides a conscience clause for medical professionals, stating that no doctor can be forced against their will to undertake an abortion procedure.

Medical practitioners on the ground, however, tell me that there is a growing tendency to ask doctors to justify their unwillingness to perform abortions. Some doctors and nurses fear that this conscience clause is under threat, and that the current climate of contracted service could see doctors having to perform abortions if they wish to remain part of the NHS.

There are now very few pro-life gynaecologists working in the Health Service, and even fewer who reach the top of their profession. Many Christian doctors don't want to specialise in gynaecology because they know that refusal to perform abortions will create serious professional difficulties.

There have been recent attempts to dismantle the conscience clause for pharmacists who are expected to sell the 'morning-after pill' over the counter. Newly qualified pharmacists are likely to find it very difficult to get work if they are pro-life and unwilling to dispense some of these increasingly popular drugs.

Many healthcare professionals are faced with such difficult issues every day. They need our prayers that God will give them both wisdom and grace. It's crucial that they offer the kind of support, compassion and resources which people need. It's also important that they are able to live with their conscience, and to practise medicine without losing the integrity of their Christian faith.

The tide turns?

Some pro-life campaigners believe that the tide is beginning to turn. Technological advances like four-dimensional ultrasound, enabling us to see live images of the child in the womb are making people more aware of the reality of life. As we learn more about the personality and characteristics of the developing foetus, with media reportage of examples such as that of an unborn twin leaning across to kiss the cheek of her sister, it will become harder and harder to consider the foetus as a disposable 'it'. These recent compelling images of the relationship of twins before birth are powerful influencers of public opinion.

The bewildering scenario of doctors in one operating theatre destroying one foetus, whilst next door others are fighting to save another that may be even younger, throws into question the whole practice of abortion, and as technological advance continually extends clinical possibilities, the frequency of these terrible contrasting scenarios increases.

It seems incredible to me that, today, one of the most

dangerous places to live on earth is in the womb of your mother! This should be the most hallowed and safe place in all the earth to be, and it seems that those whose lives are terminated have been accorded no voice in law and no rights in society. These are the most vulnerable ones among us, and I believe with my whole heart that Christ calls us to speak up for them, to defend them and to protect them. It seems to me as though God placed the new life there, within the mother's womb, because He trusted us – because He knew that there the child would be protected, cherished and kept safe. The abortion statistics of 2006, even allowing for those tragic circumstances when any woman might have felt an abortion to be necessary, represent a betrayal of trust – not only the unborn child's trust in us, but a betrayal of God's trust in us too.

Discussion Questions

1 A termination often signals some kind of personal tragedy. What kind of tragedies might drive people to seek an abortion?

   Jeremiah 1:5 states 'Before I formed you in the womb I knew you', and Psalm 139 reminds us that 'Thou didst form my inward parts, thou didst knit me together in my mother's womb, Thou knowest me right well ... my frame was not hidden from thee when I was being made in secret.' What do these passages tell us about the foetus?

2 Pro-choice campaigners have defended passionately a woman's right to choose what happens to her own body and in her own life. How would you arbitrate between the right of the baby to live, and the right of the mother over her body?

3 What do you feel have been the positive achievements in society of the Abortion Act, and what have been the negative effects? To what extent do you think the Act is interpreted and employed today in the spirit of its original intentions?

4 Over 6.2 million unborn babies have been terminated in Britain since the Abortion Act was passed. What does this figure signify to you?

5 Ground 'C' allowed abortion where: 'The continuance of the pregnancy would involve risk, greater than if the pregnancy were terminated, of injury to the physical or mental health of the pregnant woman.' How flexibly do you feel this clause should be interpreted? What examples can you imagine of 'injury to mental health'?

6 Christians have a pastoral responsibility to care for women seeking support before, during or after an abortion. Christ calls us to be present in these situations rather than absent; and to be loving rather than judgmental. What might this mean in practice?

7 'Many Christian doctors don't want to specialise in gynaecology because they know that refusal to perform abortions will create serious professional difficulties.' Why might we wish to encourage Christians to go into this field?

8 'The bewildering scenario of doctors in one operating theatre destroying one foetus, whilst next door others are fighting to save another that may be even younger ...' Explore how you feel about late abortion, compared with how you feel about early abortion. And the morning after pill? What are the differences between the ethical dilemmas they may represent?

Chapter Nine

Doing the Right Thing in Death

Withdrawing treatment

One sunny summer evening I sat at the bedside of a member of my church as he signed the permission form for relatively routine surgery. We were in a major teaching hospital, and the doctor was assuring him that 'this time tomorrow you'll be feeling much better.'

The surgery went horribly wrong, and the next evening I was holding his hand as he struggled for life. His breathing was shallow and it was supported by a life support system. I was seated beside him in the most hi-tech single unit intensive care ward that I've ever seen.

Two nurses were caring for him, and although he was completely paralysed they told me that he was still able to hear. The only way he could show his distress was to sweat.

In that hell between life and death I stayed with him but I will never forget those long dark hours of waiting, searching my heart and my faith and trying to understand. I prayed that the Lord would either heal him or release him.

As I tried to sleep in the chair by his bed that night, the hiss and thud of the respirator filled the air. His loved ones and I shared a slow-motion nightmare until, at last, the following morning the doctor called us into the Sister's office, and explained that he recommended that the treatment should cease. He advised us that the patient's level of brain activity indicated that the prognosis was poor. The doctor wanted the family (after discussion with me, their 'spiritual advisor') to give permission to withdraw treatment.

The young doctor was sensitive to the raw emotions that the family were feeling, and left the room while the family and I discussed the situation. When he returned we were all of one mind. None of us wanted to see the patient suffer like this for a moment longer than was deemed necessary.

We returned to the intensive care suite and whispered our tearful goodbyes. The doctor came in, stood quietly for a while, and then flicked the switches of the life support system, and the room went silent. We held hands and prayed, and soon my friend drifted slowly away. I commended him to the God of all mystery, and we waited for some time, speaking to him in comforting whispers, until we were sure that he was gone.

At the end, the quality of his life was so severely diminished that it was barely measurable. With no medical prospect of improvement there seemed no alternative but to withdraw treatment. The grave sense of responsibility that we shared when we became part of this decision process made a lasting and formative impact upon me.

I had no qualm of conscience about the decisions which were made in this situation. It seemed to me that medical science was keeping him alive, but that, in reality, he had no life at all. My friend was relying on us to let him go.

It was an experience which highlighted some of the central issues of the euthanasia debate for me. I recognised that there is a world of difference between keeping someone alive and killing them, between withdrawal of treatment and actively offering euthanasia.

What is euthanasia?

The word 'euthanasia' simply means 'dying well'. Over the years the dictionary definition has shifted towards becoming a technical term for mercy killing, or for assisted suicide.

We've got used to this kind of practice in animal medicine,

so that, for example, when a cat gets a fatal disease we ask the vet to put our pet out of its misery. It seems the most compassionate thing to do.

When a human life is nearing its end, where the process of dying is likely to be protracted, and either very painful or otherwise intensely distressing as, for example, dying from motor-neurone disease may sometimes be, some argue that the most loving and helpful thing to do is to support expressed wishes by the suffering person to cut the process of dying short.

So, is there anything wrong with accelerating a patient's death if it is done painlessly? Those who support euthanasia believe that there are situations where it's acceptable to help people to die and they advocate the use of drugs which, whilst giving pain relief, will also hasten death.

I believe that life is a gift from God, and that suicide – even assisted suicide under medical supervision – is against the teaching of the Christian faith and a sin against God's divine will and purposes. It is, of course, also against the law in many countries. It's one thing to believe this, however, but it is quite another to hold on to these principles when a close friend or relative is suffering intolerable agony, facing death without dignity, or languishing in a state of terminal dementia. None of us knows when we might face these issues, and it's important to think them through outside the immediacy of a family crisis.

Why is life sacred?

Jesus once said 'Aren't five sparrows sold for two pennies? Yet not one sparrow is forgotten by God. Even the hairs of your head have all been counted. So do not be afraid: you are worth much more than many sparrows!' (Luke 12:6, TEV).

Jesus made it clear that just one life – indeed EVERY life – is unique and precious to God. Human life is never

191

valueless or unimportant; it is always a gift from God, and must always be treated as priceless.

When Jesus told the story of the lost sheep, and of the good shepherd who goes off looking for it, no matter what the personal cost, He identified the inordinate value of each individual life.

To God, human life is never quantified in millions; it is always about His love for individuals. Jesus made it clear that God loves each of us and that His call is to 'love my neighbour as myself'.

Most Christians believe that to kill another human being, even when our motive is mercy, is a grievous denial of God's gift of life and a direct contradiction of the commandment, 'Thou shalt not kill.' It amounts to the destruction of a unique human being whom God has created.

I am convinced that once this moral threshold is crossed in British law, we will have lost touch with the sacred value of life. We'll have made murder legal, and unleashed on the world the kind of destructive forces that will change the foundations of our society and of our legal system.

The Christian leader Dame Cicely Saunders, who founded the modern hospice movement, discovered that good nursing and compassionate care can transform the feelings of the terminally ill and give them a rich quality of life. When she reflected on her extensive experience of caring for the dying she once remarked:

> Once pain and the feeling of isolation had been relieved they never asked for euthanasia again ... Anything that says to the very ill or the very old that there is no longer anything that matters in their life would be a deep impoverishment to society.

We live in a 'disposable' society. White goods, electronic devices, cars and clothes are bought and discarded at an increasingly rapid rate. This throw-away mentality has little

patience with repairing things which are
their sell-by date, or for valuing that whi

This attitude that regards everything
can also creep into our thinking about
such as the very ill or the elderly. The
beauty in our society can taint our view of the old a
us callous and hard-hearted towards those who are
chronically sick or disabled.

In a world dominated by bottom-line economics and
budget driven social services, it's easy to come to regard the
most vulnerable members of our society as a liability or even
as a waste of space.

If people were just sophisticated animals then perhaps
euthanasia would be a logical way forward. But human
beings are made in God's image, and the human spirit marks
us out as different from the animals. If we choose to termi-
nate the life of a human being we destroy that mysterious
spark which is a sacred gift of God.

As a church minister it has been my awesome privilege to
spend many night watches with those on the verge of death.
I haven't found this kind of Christian service easy.
Sometimes the hours of pacing hospital corridors or of sitting by the bedsides of the dying have seemed to last for an
eternity.

There have been occasions when the opportunity to
accompany someone on their last journey has been incredi-
bly precious. When you pray with someone as they slip away
it is a spiritual experience like no other. You can't help but
believe in the mystery of the human spirit and the reality of
life beyond death.

I believe that dignity in dying is not about lethal injec-
tions, but about a quality of nursing care which makes dying
one of life's most rewarding experiences. I believe that
euthanasia is wrong, and should always be unnecessary with
effective pain relief and expert palliative care. We need to
learn again that someone who is dying is of incalculable

ᴐ God and we need to communicate this sense of
to the one who is on the threshold of eternity.

Palliative care

It is little wonder that people who are suffering excruciating
pain say that they want to die. If you have to watch a loved
one enduring such agony it can shred you emotionally. Such
experiences can make euthanasia look like the best way forward and even persuade us that by prolonging life we are
contradicting the purposes of God.

Over the last thirty years there have been extensive
advances in pain control and in palliative care. Palliative
care consultants tell me that there is no medical reason why
anyone should suffer intolerable pain or discomfort at the
end of their life. Even in the most extreme cases it is
possible to sedate the patient into unconsciousness.

Christians should have no qualms in using what God has
given the medical profession to alleviate the suffering of
human beings. God has given medical science some amazing
ways of dealing with pain. The morphine produced from a
poppy, for example, fits neatly into that receptor in the brain
which controls pain.

It is because of financial restrictions in the medical service that the best care is not always made available. Some
hospitals have prioritised their other services above palliative care, and in some areas it has become under-resourced
and as a result some patients are suffering a completely
unnecessary kind of death. Pain is the budget option – and
this is something we can change.

Good palliative care will eradicate a patient's desire to end
it all. Key aspects of it involve making the patient feel
comfortable and giving them back a sense of dignity and personal control. Patients often feel very depressed when they
no longer feel that they are in control of their lives, but good
palliative care can successfully restore this. Expert nursing

and compassionate support are crucial in ensuring that terminal illness is never too much to bear. It is also important that helpless people understand clearly that they are not a nuisance to their carers, since this is an issue that weighs heavily on the minds of people who have been highly responsible and independent prior to their illness.

I fear that if euthanasia were to be introduced as a legal option then palliative care would all but disappear from the medical profession. Hospitals would refuse to invest money in professional expertise, drugs and quality nursing for the terminally ill if instead they had the option of paying for just one lethal injection to end a person's life. The cost effectiveness of euthanasia would quickly diminish our compassionate care for the dying.

I believe that the ideals of the healthcare profession would be tarnished if employees became involved in the termination of their patients. The core values of the medical vocation which prize the best care of the patient and the sanctity of life would be permanently devalued.

Christians should have nothing to do with euthanasia. Instead we should be at the forefront of palliative care, and become more aware of how financial cut-backs are affecting the quality of treatment of the terminally ill. We all have a responsibility to ensure that the dying receive the drugs and support they need. We must do everything that we can to argue that, even in a cash-starved health service, death should be pain free, and that palliative care is an important aspect of any civilised health service.

Suicide and assisted suicide

Many believe that it's acceptable to deny food and water to those who have only days to live, and that this should be regarded as the 'withdrawal of treatment'. They argue that, in this situation, the doctor is simply allowing nature to take its course. I find such a practice morally and ethically questionable, and believe that it undermines the value of human life.

Some say that the removal of food and fluids can itself create suffering whilst others argue that by continuing to give them, we only make death more prolonged and uncomfortable. This food and fluidscontroversy remains a grey area, with some of those who oppose euthanasia feeling that it represents a policy of terminating life by another name. Some doctors who do not advocate euthanasia point out that some patients who are very close to death 'turn their face to the wall' anyway, and don't want any food or water.

They suggest that the cessation of food and fluids, when judged correctly, can be seen as just a stage in the process of dying.

It is also the case that oral administration of fluids can actually hasten death. If a patient whose ability to swallow is compromised is given a drink, there is a high risk of fluid entering the lungs and triggering the onset of pneumonia. This is a common occurrence.

There can be little doubt that some doctors employ the removal of food and fluids as a legal means of hastening death. I personally struggle with this practice, and was uncomfortable when I witnessed it first hand during the death of a close relative. The doctor explained that he had previously discussed different options with the patient, and that by denying food and fluids he was simply fulfilling the patient's wishes. I didn't contradict him at the time, but in retrospect I wish that I had asked more searching questions of him.

Nursing staff say that a death hastened by dehydration is a distressing way to die but that's hard to prove in the case of people too helpless to signal distress. Ultimately, I'm not convinced that the denial of food and fluids is integral to good nursing practice or to truly compassionate care. It should be borne in mind too, that once a patient has reached this stage, there is not much further to go; they are already dying. It seems wisest then, to simply make them comfortable in whatever way the body needs, so that the natural experience of death may be dignified, peaceful and free of distress.

The withholding of food and fluids under some circumstances (such as when a patient is fully conscious) is, in my opinion, assisted suicide, and may even be abusive. I see it as legally questionable and regard it as a practice which sets dangerous precedents.

Leslie Burke has a progressive degenerative disease and is now in a wheelchair. He became deeply concerned that he would reach a point in his disease when he would be too weak to feed himself, so Leslie used the law to try to ensure that he was not denied food and fluids in the terminal stages of his illness.

The court ruled against him, stating that decisions about food and fluids should ultimately be made by the doctors supervising his case. This was a legal ruling which many who oppose euthanasia consider to be a mistake with tragic long term consequences for future patients.

Diane Pretty, on the other hand, went to court to apply for assisted suicide. She felt, because she was physically incapable of committing suicide herself, she was denied a basic human right which healthy human beings can exercise at will.

The court decided that, by receiving assistance in committing suicide she would be making another person complicit in her murder, and so this permission was denied.

Joni Earickson Tada, the American author with an international ministry to the physically challenged, has lived a dynamic and full life – even though she is paralysed from the neck down. Christine Owen, who won the Whitbread Prize for literature, used the award ceremony to make it clear that, although she is paralysed from the neck down, this does not give other people the right to comment on the quality or worth of her life.

These cases make apparent to us that, whether healthy,

sick, dying or disabled, people retain their individual preferences, their spirit and personality, everything that makes
them real people. It is important we bear this in mind in our
dealings with people who appear to us to have a very poor
quality of life, especially where their ability to communicate
is impaired.

One of the important contributions of the hospice movement to this debate has been the discovery that with good
palliative care support, the desire to cut life short often melts
away. Surprisingly, it is actually a common phenomenon to
find hospice patients averring that they would not have
missed this stretch of their lives for the world – even that
they felt they never really lived until now. In His love, it
seems Christ still often saves the best wine for the end of the
party. This being the case, it seems that the question of
euthanasia should not even be raised, let alone considered,
until everything possible has been done, not to artificially
extend life in a dying person but to support and promote the
peace of body and soul during the sacred time of a human
being's last days on this earth.

An ethical minefield

Once the moral threshold which considers life to be sacred
has been passed, I believe that the legal safeguards protecting life would quickly be eroded. As we have seen with the
wording of Ground C in the abortion legislation, what at first
appeared a tightly defined legal safeguard quickly became
practically meaningless.

If euthanasia were to be restricted to those who were
deemed mentally competent, how would that be defined?
What raft of legal safeguards would we need to put in place
to ensure that the patient's best interests were always
preserved? Is it not possible that in the future some health
service manager under massive pressure to remove a 'bed

blocker' might be tempted to interpret mental competence to suit their own financial agenda?

If two men were lying next to each other in hospital with exactly the same illness, but one had his full mental faculties whilst the other was mentally incapacitated, which one should be euthanised? The one who is aware of what is going on around him or the one who is mentally incapacitated?

According to Dutch law, euthanasia can be offered only to the one who is mentally alert, but I believe it's only a matter of time before budget starved Dutch hospitals demand that the law extends to the other patient too. In practice one set of decisions quickly affects others.

If the Dutch law were to be extended to cover the mentally incompetent, I believe that this could lead to some of the most vulnerable people in our society being euthanised. Who would make choices on their behalf, and how could we be sure that such choices were made legally? What family conflicts might this occasion? In all the turmoil of decision-making, signing forms, seeking permission, making arrangements, implementing medical processes – what would become of the opportunity to sit quietly with dying people, hold their hands and pray for them, assure them they are loved, in this fleeting, precious ending time of a life?

If families were to be involved in the decision-making processes about euthanasia, are there not dangers that personal financial considerations might play a part? The vast costs of care homes or nursing services might mean that some families could be convinced that a lethal injection would be 'in everyone's interests'.

There is some evidence that in Holland, where about 9,000 patients are euthanised each year, some elderly people are becoming fearful of their doctors and even of their relatives. Indeed, there are reports that some elderly Dutch patients are travelling to Germany for medical treatment to escape the implications of this practice of euthanasia in their own country.

To me, what is happening in Holland represents the thin end of the wedge. Once the practice of euthanasia is established, it won't be long before those with psychiatric problems, younger children with serious medical conditions and those with non-acute terminal illnesses will be given the opportunity to die.

The opportunity to give a lethal injection to someone requesting it opens up a minefield of issues for doctors to evaluate. Many patients go through dark and depressing experiences as part of difficult and sometimes debilitating treatment; it's hardly surprising that they go through days when they feel they've had enough. But those who might opt for suicide one day do sometimes feel very differently the next. Upon which day's perspective should we act? How on earth can such a decision-making process be properly safe-guarded or policed?

Most Christians believe that life is given by God and that God should decide when it ends. If we make it the norm to decide for ourselves when we will die, we usurp the divine prerogative, and take our destiny into our own hands.

Once this kind of personal autonomyabout death becomes normal practice it must surely follow that suicide will become socially acceptable.

People who are feeling depressed could then seek the legal option of assisted suicide. Many people can testify that it was out of the darkest hours of their lives that unexpected oppor-tunity and new hope grew. The legal provision of assisted suicide (which would no doubt become somebody's wonder-ful commercial opportunity) would create the likelihood of individuals reacting to the winter-times of life without ever giving themselves the chance to see the returning spring. Given the numbers of people in our society who are cur-rently receiving anti-depressant medication, it seems the death rate might be expected to rise significantly.

In a society that became acculturated to the norm of death being planned and decided, it naturally follows that we would stop treating the hundreds of people who take drug overdoses every year, and stop sending police officers to talk people down from jumping off high buildings. In such a society the thousands of people who have attempted suicide, but who have survived and lived to regret their actions, would never be given such a second chance. Such a form of personal autonomy has far-reaching implications for the future of humanity.

The increasing popularity of living wills, known in law as 'advanced directives', is an important aspect of this ethical issue. Living wills give us the opportunity to specify what level of treatment we would accept in various future health scenarios that we might face.

The drawback with these advance directives is that it's impossible to know how you will actually feel in the situations which you might list, or what the particulars of the actual scenario might be. If you had stipulated that you wanted no further treatment after a stroke, it's impossible to predict just what the after-effects of such a stroke might be, or how you might feel when you had to face that situation. Those who have watched loved ones suffer the after-effects of stroke may with good reason wish to avoid a similar experience. One of the difficulties here, however, is that it's hard to say whether withholding treatment will have the effect of saving you from disablement by allowing you to die, or of condemning you to disablement because you didn't die, and the treatment would have enhanced recovery.

Advanced directives also impose the ethical preferences of individuals upon the group who deliver their care in event of incapacity. Lawyers predict a glut of new cases involving the relatives of patients who want to revoke the living wills of their loved ones. Although autonomy sounds good, it can lead to many difficult moral and ethical dilemmas.

Euthanasia is not the way forward. Prohibition of intentional killing has been part of the glue that has bound our society together for many hundreds of years and it's at the foundation of criminal law itself.

At present the law of England is perfectly clear. If you kill someone intentionally you are guilty of murder, but if you are simply alleviating pain, and a patient dies, you are not guilty of murder. If we change the law on intentional killing we erode something which is deeply significant to the whole structure of our society and to the immense value which we put on human life.

Chronic degenerative disease

Over the last decade or so the debate on euthanasia has shifted. It used to focus on the right of cancer patients to die because of their pain and discomfort. Advances in cancer treatment and pain relief have weakened this argument, however, and most of the recent cases coming to law involve patients with chronic degenerative diseases of one kind or another.

The argument for euthanasia is that patients should have the right to choose how and when they die. They should not have to wait for an illness such as motor neuron disease to take its course. It's a quest for choice, with the patient preferring to die from a lethal injection rather than from some distressing or prolonged symptom of their disease.

The vast majority of disabled people and disability rights groups remain opposed to euthanasia, however. One of the concerns of the disability support group Radar is that disabled people require protection. If euthanasia became the norm in our society, disabled people fear that they might fall victim to a doctor who assessed their life as simply not worth living, while their own view of their situation might be considerably different.

This kind of anxiety among disabled or chronically sick patients is not as far-fetched as it might sound. Several years ago I was supporting the family of a seriously ill patient with a chronic degenerative disease in a hospital at about 2am one morning. I overheard a deeply disturbing discussion between two young doctors which focused on the concept that sometimes life is not worth living. They were wondering whether the time had come to discontinue treatment for my friend. Thankfully, that option was not pursued, and some five years later my friend is enjoying an excellent quality of life; but it opened my eyes to the stark reality of this kind of situation.

Discussion Questions

1   Have you ever accompanied someone on the journey of dying? What helped to support you, and them, and what was unhelpful?

2   What are your own views about euthanasia and assisted suicide? What have been the experiences in your life that led you to these conclusions?

3   What has your experience of the hospice movement been? What do you understand to be the difference in terms of quality of life and ethics between euthanasia (that brings about death in a peaceful way) and palliative care (that offers treatment which will not prolong life but will make a dying person comfortable)?

4   What are your thoughts ... fears ... experiences ... concerning chronic degenerative disease or disability? Which aspects do you feel you could face with equanimity, and what would cause you serious distress?

5   If you decided to write a letter for your relatives and carers to read in the event of illness (perhaps a stroke) that made you helpless and unable to speak, what would you include in your letter?

6   In what ways do you feel that the issues of abortion and euthanasia are related, and in what ways do they address very different issues?

7   When someone is disabled, dying, or chronically infirm, they rely on other people to implement their wishes and help them exercise choices. What scenarios can you imagine where a conflict of moral values within this group of people creates an ethical dilemma?

Chapter Ten

Doing the Right Thing in Society

The world of politics

Each of us has the potential to shape the society of which we're a part. This starts with taking care of ourselves, so that we will not be a burden to others, and so that we are happy people who can lift the hearts of those we meet. Then it spreads to taking care of our loved ones, those who are close to us, whose happiness God has especially entrusted to our care. If they are encouraged and affirmed, and feel sure they are loved, if they set out each morning from a home that is a sanctuary and a nurturing, cherishing place, they will spread the light of love and make the world a better place. But God's call upon our lives does not stop there.

Nothing was ever changed by those who cared only about themselves. It is important that we look beyond our own lives and households, not only to include those among our neighbours who are lonely and struggling, but to fulfil our responsibility as citizens. We didn't come here just to get what we could for ourselves and leave the rest. Part of our calling as Christians is to work tirelessly in partnership with God's love, expressed in the renewal of creation, the work of reconciliation, and the redeeming of the world.

Recent research in the UK has demonstrated that committed Christians are offering a wonderful witness to God's love in their communities by serving others in very practical ways. If you took all the Christians out of health, education, law, youth work and the voluntary sector, many of these key elements of social care would be seriously weakened. Most Christians recognise God's call to make the world a better place.

It's an integral part of the Christian vocation, and an important expression of our faith. Many Christians are involved in working with asylum seekers, caring for the homeless, helping the elderly, or supporting young offenders. Practical involvement in the local community has always been seen as a necessary expression of faith.

Christians also need to catch the vision that they can not only help and encourage and serve, but actually transform and influence the society of which they are a part. Our faith is expressed in kindness to those we meet along the way, but also in questioning and challenging the policies of government, holding our political leaders to account, and doing all that is in our power to uphold and preserve the values, traditions, laws and practices that promote the wellbeing of creation and human society, and that are honouring to God.

Each vocation is unique and related to the temperament and circumstances of the individual, and the Christian sense of mission should always be motivated by love and energised by joy rather than driven by guilt; but as all Christians benefit from being part of the infrastructure of a wider society, so all must contribute towards shaping and determining what the quality of that social framework will be.

Organisations such as the Evangelical Alliance, Care and Transform UK have mobilised thousands of Christians to join campaigns which aim to shape the direction of government policy. Over recent years there have been petitions, parliamentary lobbies, marches and public meetings. It seems as if the people of God are on the march again!

Not all Christians feel comfortable with this kind of activity, however. They look to the teaching of Paul and Peter that Christians should support the government in power at all times. They feel very uncomfortable with the idea of questioning those in power or of getting involved in a public demo.

Over the last fifty years Christians have not usually been at the forefront of engagement, either at a scholarly or a practical level, with the big issues of their day. Some have questioned whether Christians should care about such issues at all, and have expressed fears that such a social gospel may not be sound. There is a significant proportion of the faith community, and indeed the wider community, who believe firmly that it is wrong to mix politics with religion.

Sceptics like these suggest that in 1 Timothy 2:1–4, Titus 3:1 and 1 Peter 2:13–17 the church's emphasis was on respect for law and order, constructive citizenship, and on the prayerful support of civic authorities.

They point out that in Romans 13:1–7 Paul actually counsels Christians that submission to the governing authorities is God's will, on the basis that they have been instituted by God and act as God's servants in executing 'wrath on the wrongdoer' and extracting due taxes from their citizens.

But the Revd Dr John Stott has highlighted the need for Christians to develop a 'Christian mind ... which can think with Christian integrity about the problems of the contemporary world.' I'm convinced that he's right, and that we're entering a new season in which Christians are beginning to engage with the political agenda again.

'When people say the Bible and politics don't mix,' says Archbishop Desmond Tutu, 'I don't know which Bible they are referring to. It's not the one I've been reading.'

Reacting to the verses in Romans 13, the Bible scholar J.C. O'Neill suggested that these seven verses 'have caused more unhappiness and misery in the Christian East and West than any other seven verses in the New Testament'. Many scholars agree that 'submission' in this passage must mean more than mere uncritical subjection or obedience.

C.E.B. Cranfield concludes that 'Paul is enjoining ... no uncritical obedience to whatever command the civil authority may decide to give, but the recognition that one has been placed below the authority of God'.

Cranfield goes on to stress that the Christian's subjection to the authorities is limited to respecting them, obeying them in so far as such obedience does not conflict with God's laws, and 'seriously and responsibly disobeying them when it does'.

The Revd Dr David Hillborn has done some excellent theological work to support this Christian involvement in social change. He concludes that most serious Bible scholars cite Acts 5:29 as support for the view that proper interpretation of this passage implies that 'We must obey God rather than persons!'

Hillborn suggests that the proper interpretation of these passages means that Christians should not sit in quiet complicity when a government implements policies which are counter to the purposes of God.

I'm convinced that Christian commitment to the will of God always over-rides their obedience to the state. And I'm really encouraged that in recent years many Christians have taken to the streets in peaceful if noisy protest to oppose government policy when they have perceived that such policy runs counter to the will of God.

Last year marked 200 years since William Wilberforce won the fight to abolish slavery by changing the law in the British parliament. In the years that followed, hundreds of thousands of slaves were released from bondage around the world.

This aspect of Wilberforce's political activity was just a small aspect of his long term Christian commitment to social change. Wilberforce's work was not single issue-politics; he was committed to a 40 year campaign to change the mindset of the nation on a range of issues.

The Clapham Sect, to which Wilberforce belonged, recognised that slavery was only one component of a set of national moral and spiritual values which urgently needed to be challenged if they were to bring social practice in line with biblical values.

Initially Wilberforce's strategy was to work through Parliament. He used a top-down strategy. But after many frustrating attempts to change the law on slavery he had to face up to the fact that this simply did not work.

Wilberforce changed to a bottom-up strategy. He began to use the multitude of voluntary associations that he and other members of the Clapham Sect had formed, especially those with a missionary emphasis such as the Church Missionary Society and the British & Foreign Bible Society, to seed a new kind of 'people movement' for social change.

These voluntary organisations had local groups throughout the country and Wilberforce mobilised their members to sign the petition bearing more than half a million signatures in support of his anti-slavery campaign. He presented this petition to the House of Commons to great effect. In a total population of just over 9 million this 500,000 signatures was an impressive demonstration of people power.

Many historians view this as the first mobilisation of grassroots support for a social campaign in British history. Wilberforce had discovered that a top-down political strategy could be far more effective for social change if it was supported by a bottom-up people movement involving hundreds of thousands of ordinary voters.

I'm convinced that now, more than ever, Christians should be actively following and questioning government policy. And where they feel that it contradicts the values of their faith they should feel free to speak out about it and actively try to change it.

This reactive model is very much the second-best way of working, however. If we are to effectively emulate the vision of Wilberforce and the Clapham Sect we should be proactively creating public opinion, not reacting to it. We should be involved in forming government policy as well as offering our critique on what already exists.

The Evangelical Alliance has published two thought-provoking papers in support of this kind of action. They are called 'Uniting for Change: An Evangelical Vision for Transforming Society' and 'Movement for Change: Evangelical Perspectives for Transforming Society'. Both of these important papers set out the rationale for a movement for change rooted in an understanding of the kingdom of God at work in society.

Christians are beginning to address public issues in a more considered manner and are seeking ways of applying biblical principles to specific societal contexts. This process has been described as engaging in public theology, a term defined by the Lutheran social ethicist Dr Robert Benne as 'the engagement of a living religious tradition with its public environment'.

The vision of Care in raising up a team of young Christians to work as researchers in the British Parliament is an effective illustration of Benne's definition. It's been my privilege to get to know some of them. As they immerse themselves in the cut and thrust of political life on all sides of the political spectrum, they gain understanding of the political system and insights into how it might be influenced. Many of them will acquire the skills to become successful politicians themselves and hopefully will begin to shape the political agenda in the years to come.

God is calling us to change society, to advocate our biblical worldview, and to influence public policy. Our Christian faith inspires us to take note of what Scripture says and to emphasise its primary authority, and it also challenges us to become much more knowledgeable and concerned about contemporary social issues.

This book is designed to stimulate the kind of Christian involvement which gets you thinking about the kind of world you want to live in. This last chapter should not be an ending, but a beginning. It's about encouraging you to identify the things about which you feel strongly, inspiring the motivation to see real change in these situations.

The world of business

Wilberforce's campaign against slavery was successful, but it wasn't the end of the story. Today, experts estimate that there are still over 12 million people who are enslaved in some way. They may not be shipped in chains like the slaves of the 17th century were, but they are still people with a price on their head. They are human beings, bought and sold like products in the market place and with no freedom to make their own way in the world.

This is a global trade. Children are bought and sold to work in the sari industry in India. Young boys are sold to serve on fishing boats in Ghana. Some girls under ten years of age are kept in brothels in Cambodia. Filipino women are trafficked as domestic helps, and find themselves being used as prostitutes with no rights and no income.

Countries like Great Britain aren't exempt from this dreadful trafficking. Chinese workers are up to their waists in mud in the cockle picking industry, Russian women are trafficked into the country illegally to serve as prostitutes, and peasants from European countries are kept in intolerable conditions for work in harvest fields.

All this is slavery by a different name, even if desperation for money or a fresh start has forced these workers into voluntary agreements. It's a tragedy that these practices still exist in the modern world.

It all started when a man called John Hawkins sold 200 slaves to the planters in Haiti. Recently I visited Haiti, and I was astonished to discover that children called 'restavecs' are still used as child labour, with no rights or pay, right now on that same island.

Christians believe that every human being is unique and precious to God. We were given life so that we might be free, not so that we might be bought and sold as cheap merchandise. Christians must play a full part in the global movement to stop the trafficking of human beings today. We need to challenge the use of anyone as free labour and to stop those who deny the basic human rights of another human being. And we must oppose the evil and despicable trade in children, and the exploitative horrors of the sex industry.

I was shocked and disappointed to learn that John Newton, the author of the great hymn Amazing Grace, continued to serve in the slave trade for about five years after he became a Christian. He was a man of his time, and the prevalent Christian culture of his day was that slavery was acceptable and that buying and selling human beings was an integral part of God's will.

It's so easy for us to be blinded by the sinful practices of our contemporary world just as John Newton was in his day. We can easily absorb the attitudes of those around us to such an extent that we can't see clearly how our business practices are hurting others.

John Newton, as a Christian, looked to the Bible and found there the texts that encouraged him to believe his practice of slave-trading was acceptable. What is necessary for us as biblical Christians is to read the Bible in the wholeness of its message – not winkling out little proof texts to support our own interest and agenda, but so that God's Spirit may transform us by the renewing of our minds.

The mean and selfish attitudes which lay behind slavery are still around in some workplaces today. We can still regard others as having less value than ourselves. We can still abuse our power over other workers, disregard them, or use them for our own financial gain.

Ultimately God wants us to serve others, not to dominate them. He wants us to love them, not to use them; to set them free, not to abuse them. Our attitudes towards others reveal the truth about our Christian commitment and indicate whether we have really grasped the message of God's love for all.

In our working lives many of us hire and fire, manage teams, lead organisations or exert power and influence.

What would Jesus do in such a privileged position? I'm convinced that he'd find ways of empowering others, of affirming them and of making the workplace full of life, love and compassion.

If we are to work in business as followers of Jesus, we must ensure that those with whom we work are energised and released by the creativity of their work, not destroyed by its tedium or repetition. Christians in positions of management have a responsibility toward those who work with them to ensure that they reach their full potential and are not cramped and limited by fear and boredom.

Health

Thousands of Christians serve Christ in the Health Service, but many of those I meet feel powerless and frustrated by the kind of management culture in which they work. They tell me that they often feel trapped by the budget-driven agenda which makes it hard to keep on caring.

The Hippocratic oath originated in the school of medicine founded by Hippocrates (born 460 BCE) on the island of Kos. The oath was taken on graduation from medical school and it gave a kind of benchmark for how doctors should behave and how they should care for their patients. Medical graduates no longer automatically swear this oath, but in the United States about 98 per cent still choose to do so, while in the UK the proportion is about 50 percent.

The principles enshrined in the Hippocratic oath are still very much part of contemporary medical practice. Part of the British Medical Association's interpretation of the oath reads:

I recognise the special value of human life but I also know that the prolongation of human life is not the only aim of healthcare. I will use my training and professional standing to improve the community in which I work. I will treat patients equitably and support a fair and humane distribution of health resources.

But what does that actually mean today, when the financial bottom line often seems to take the highest priority? Any health service that is completely utilitarian, or driven by financial goals can produce only inferior results. As a Christian, I believe that the best health professionals must have a sense of the transcendent.

They need to recognise that they are not just performing clinical procedures, but are dealing with real human beings. They are not just meeting budgetary targets, but treating patients with compassion and care. They are not just trying to save time, but are generous in spending whatever time is necessary.

A nurse friend of mine went to work with Mother Theresa. One smelly, wasted dying man was brought into her hospice late one night. Mother Theresa pressed my friend close to him and wrapped her arms around his withered body. 'Love until it hurts', she whispered.

It was reminiscent of what the famous doctor Thomas Sydenham once wrote: 'The doctor must one day give an account to the Supreme Judge of all the lives entrusted to his care. The doctor's skill, and knowledge, and energy as they have been given by God, should be exercised for God's glory, and the good of mankind, and not for mere gain or ambition. The doctor should reflect that he has undertaken the care of no mean creature, for, in order that he may estimate the value, the greatness of the human race, the only begotten Son of God became himself a man, and thus ennobled it with his divine dignity, and far more than this, died to redeem it.'

Christian health workers must catch the vision of serving with real compassion, and cultivate a rock solid commitment to care that goes far beyond the expectations of the systems which so constrain them.

We pray that God will raise up more Christian doctors and nurses of vision and commitment, and that a new generation of medical leaders might bring a greater sense of the transcendent into the wards and surgeries of our health service.

Without this, the clinical practice of medicine is no longer healing, but becomes purely mechanistic; and patients are not machines but intricately made individuals who have been created in the precious image of God.

Law

Over recent years it's been my privilege to meet many Christians who are involved in the police force, the prison service, the judiciary and legal practice. I've come to realise that this isn't an easy context in which to live a Christian life or to serve in a Christ-like way.

Around the world there are vastly different views about policing, law and order and prison. In some countries political prisoners or suspected terrorists can be held in custody for months or even years without trial. Elsewhere policing is corrupt, and many police officers and officials are open to bribery. In some places new forms of punishment are being tested, like electronic tagging, or community service. Increasingly, prisoners are being asked to say sorry to those they have hurt, and sometimes have to make direct reparation for their crimes.

It's a complicated picture. But certain guiding principles must always be at the centre of it all. How do we make the punishment fit the crime? And how can that punishment have a positive outcome for the prisoner, so that when they leave prison they don't just go back and re-offend?

Some believe that many people end up in jail for the wrong reasons. These prisoners may have psychiatric problems, have been subjected to dreadful abuse in state-run children's homes, or have known great disadvantage because they are unable to read or write.

In the UK and the USA there are often far higher numbers of black prisoners than white, and experts suggest that there might be institutional racism in the legal system which affects these figures. Prison can be the very worst place for young offenders, serving as a training school for crime rather than a place of transformation.

Police officers are often at the sharp end of this situation, finding that whatever they do, someone will think that they are in the wrong. Christians who work in this field must be prepared to confront injustice wherever it is found.

If people end up in prison because of the backgrounds they come from rather than the crimes they commit, this can't be right. Even where criminals are justly apprehended and convicted, if it is the life circumstances that nurtured them that created the end result, then imprisoning the individual makes very little difference – it is the ongoing social environment and culture that must change. Whenever we speak up for the oppressed we speak up for Jesus, and whenever we try to right wrongs that have been committed in the name of the law we speak up for God.

Christians should visit those in prison, pray for those who witness for Christ in prisons, and support those who fight for justice in the legal system and care for the victims of crime. We must stand with the vulnerable in our society, whether they be the victims of crime or the perpetrators of it. Jesus said that on the Day of Judgement he would be looking out for those who had visited him in prison!

When we visit those in prison we visit Jesus himself. When we care passionately about justice in the world we do God's work. When we look after those who have messed up their lives, and point to a new life in Christ, we share the heart of the gospel.

Defence

Sometimes in the movies the activities of war look quite glamorous. The uniforms, the fighter planes, the brave acts of heroism, the romance and often – the final victory!

Yet we only have to watch the news to see that war leads to human suffering on a massive scale. The images of children screaming with napalm burns, men searching for their loved ones in burnt-out ruins, and long lines of displaced people trudging towards refugee camps remind us of the true horrors of war.

Some Christians go to endless lengths to advocate pacifism; sometimes, like Norman Kember mentioned previously, they pay a huge personal cost in the process.

Others join the armed forces, and see their military service as an integral part of their Christian commitment and an expression of their desire to protect and defend those values which are intrinsically Christian.

On subjects like war and peace, the Bible's teaching offers guidelines, not directives. Deeply committed Christians sometimes see the same issues from diametrically opposed perspectives.

Most would agree that war is the result of sin. The apostle James wrote: 'What causes wars, and what causes fightings among you? Is it not your passions that are at war in your members?'

But there are guiding principles which all genuine Christians must share, such as love and justice. When love and justice point in the same direction it's easy to see the way ahead, but in a world of hatred and misunderstanding they are often pointing in different directions. At such times we may have to make choices as to what is the most loving way forward or the most just course of action.

Some Christians believe that human conflicts reflect the greater cosmic war which is constantly being waged between the forces of good and evil. Others hold that war itself is a component of the evil against which the good is struggling. The Bible teaches, however, that at the supernatural level the result has already been decided!

'On the cross' wrote Paul, 'Christ stripped the spiritual rulers and authorities of their power.' Christians know that at the end of world history, the Prince of Peace will reign in total triumph.

Until then, we are called to be peacemakers, and to work for forgiveness, reconciliation and peace wherever it is possible for it to be achieved.

Personal lifestyle

We are living in an age of addiction. Wherever I go in the world I hear how people simply can't live without alcohol, drugs, gambling, cigarettes, sugar, caffeine and sex.

Addictions of any kind can destroy families, careers and relationships. They jeopardise health and ruin countless millions of lives. Christians must ask, what is driving this kind of addiction? Why do human beings become so reliant on such props just to survive?

As these addictions grow out of control the consequences for individual victims and for society as a whole can be devastating, but the Christian message has news of hope for a driven and bingeing society.

The Bible teaches that 'if the Son of man shall set you free, you shall be free indeed.' But what does that actually mean, and how do we find release from enslavement to the habits and addictions that can so easily dominate our lives?

Millions of lives around the world are being destroyed by addiction. It can't be right. God didn't create us to live a life of bondage to anything or anyone other than our Saviour, Jesus Christ.

The Bible makes it clear that drunkenness is to be avoided, and that when we abuse alcohol we're neither honouring God nor caring for our bodies.

Jewish culture warned that great care should be taken over the use of alcohol. The wines of Bible times contained a low level of alcohol and weren't anywhere near as powerful as many of the drinks on sale in the pubs and bars of today.

Those of us who are Christians are called to set a personal example. Paul reminded us 'that whether you eat or drink you should do it all for the glory of God.' Our lives shouldn't be the cause for anyone to stumble.

Programmes which help people to overcome their addictions are positive and helpful, and when we totally yield our lives to Jesus Christ and are filled with the Holy Spirit, we can find a new life and a new lifestyle.

We are called to live an addiction-free lifestyle which glorifies Christ and which exemplifies a life full of the Holy Spirit. We can say all the right things, but if we are in chains to various kinds of addictions ourselves we lose the moral authority to say them.

Doing the right thing yourself

No matter how 'Christian' our views might be on the big issues covered in this book, if the way in which we live our own lives is unloving, uncaring or unforgiving then we are just being hypocritical!

We often sing the hymn Amazing Grace, but grace is a far more rich and complex gift than most of us recognise. We read in the Bible of situations in which God lets go of people, and of stories in which he even allows them to run head-long into a life of rebellion and self destruction.

In the Garden of Eden, God could have ring-fenced the Tree of Life with a hundred foot high electric fence, but instead He simply asked Adam and Eve not to eat of its fruit. He gave them free will: the right to choose, to rebel and to go their own selfish way. It's little wonder, then, that when God walked in the garden they felt so ashamed, and wanted to hide.

This kind of generous offer that allows us to choose, with no strings attached, is the hall-mark of genuine love. It is one of the ways in which we know just how much God loves us. He does not control us, like machines; he sets us free to make our own choices and to make our own mistakes.

When Jesus met the rich young ruler and offered him

salvation – the cost proved too much for him. Following Jesus involved a selfless lifestyle – and the starting point had to be the sacrifice of his wealth and position. It seemed just too great a price for him to pay. Jesus did not run after him, try to make him change his mind or beg him to think again. He simply let him go! Jesus must have been heartbroken at the choice which the rich young ruler made; but he didn't try to stop him.

As Jesus broke bread and poured wine at the Last Supper He already knew that the cross lay ahead of Him and that Judas would betray Him. Even knowing this, He still seated Judas at the seat of honour by His side, dipped bread in the bowl and offered it to him as a sign of respect, and then served him by washing his feet. At no time did Jesus beg, threaten or argue with Judas as he left the Last Supper to betray Him. He simply went on loving him. He allowed him to go out into the night, knowing full well that soon he would return to kiss Him in betrayal.

In many everyday situations we are faced with the simple choice: am I going to do God's will or my own? Am I going to live the life of love that Jesus calls me to live, or am I going to be driven by an attitude which puts me at the centre and pushes everyone else into the margin?

The most amazing thing about grace is that we are given this kind of choice at all! God did not create us to be remote-controlled robots or mindless automatons. He gave us a mind, a will and a heart and He took the risk of giving us free will.

This freedom to choose is a mark of His love for us. The hall-mark of grace is that He does not control us, but liberates us to make our own decisions and to make our own mistakes.

God's grace says 'you are free to choose your own path and to make your own mistakes. You are even free to hurt others and to live a self pre-occupied existence – you can even reject Me and turn your back on My love!'

In giving us free will, God trusts us. He reaches out to us and says 'I love you so much that I even give you the right to reject my way and to go your own way.' That really is amazing grace!

But with this grace comes an awesome responsibility. Because we have this freedom to choose, our actions betray the kind of people we are and the kind of values which we embrace.

Jesus laid great emphasis on the thoughts and feelings of his hearers. He made it clear that it wasn't good enough not to get found out, or to appear to be good. What mattered was what lay in our innermost thoughts and attitudes.

Our thought life is the source of our motives. And our motives drive our choices and actions. If my inner life is dominated by wrong thinking it will inevitably show through in my actions towards other people.

Whether it's at home, at work or in society Jesus is calling us to live lives which are pure and loving, lives which put others before ourselves, full of an inner love, which looks for no reward and which drives every aspect of who we are.

Doing the right thing flows from this love inside us. Doing the right thing flows from a life surrendered to Jesus Christ, and engenders a life that's full of the Holy Spirit.

God is looking for men and women of integrity who will live holy lives that are accountable to God and to the Body of Christ. This kind of personal integrity glorifies God, protects us from stumbling, and encourages personal growth.

One day, every secret will be made known and every decision we have made will be weighed in the great scales of God's perfect justice and Christ's perfect grace. The Christian life is life lived to the full. It's great fun. But it carries with it an awesome sense of responsibility!

Discussion Questions

1 What is the difference between 'serving society' and 'transforming society'?

2 Read Romans 13:1–7. How do you interpret this passage?

3 What should Christians do when a government implements policies which are counter to what they believe to be the purposes of God?

4 In what ways might we be forming government policy rather than satisfying ourselves with offering our critique? What kind of policies should we be advocating?

5 What public issues do you feel strongly about? What changes would you like to see in these areas? What part can you see yourself playing in bringing about such change?

6 'The mean and selfish attitudes which lay behind slavery are still around in some workplaces today.' How do they manifest themselves?

7 In our working lives many of us hire and fire, manage teams, lead organisations or exert power and influence. What would Jesus do and how would Jesus lead in such a privileged position?

8 When love and justice point in the same direction it's easy to see the way ahead, but in a world of hatred and misunderstanding they are often pointing in different directions! How do you think we should decide, if ever, that we must go to war?

9 Those of us who are Christians are called to set a personal example through our lifestyle. How do we do that?

10 Why did God give us free will – wouldn't it have been a lot easier if He'd kept control of us? What would life be like if we didn't have free will? Is free will a mixed blessing?

11 In many everyday situations we are faced with the simple choice: am I going to do God's will or my own? What kind of choices have you faced?